ISBN: 978-1-68564-853-4 (print)
ISBN: 978-1-68564-854-1 (ebook)

Printed in the U.S.A.

NOTED MEMORIES

How A Kid From Charlotte Had A Moment
With Tony, Aretha, Bonnie, Sheryl And More

BY **LARRY FARBER**

NOTED MEMORIES

Available in paperback and Kindle version for
$25 plus tax (and shipping when applicable)

- Amazon and elsewhere online.

- Park Road Books at Park Road Shopping Center, Charlotte.
  (704) 525-9239. www.parkroadbooks.com.

- Discovered Traditions Gift Shop at Temple Beth El,
  5101 Providence Road, Charlotte. (704) 749-3060.
  www.templebethel.org.

- Middle C Jazz Club, 300 S. Brevard St., uptown Charlotte.
  (704) 595-3311. www.middlecjazz.com.

- Music With Friends. (704) 607-3937. Available at each show.

- You can also email surquhsrt@middlecjazz.com to order a copy.

Partial sales from the book will support *Arts Plus*, a Charlotte-based nonprofit that sponsors arts education for students of all ages, skill levels and socioeconomic backgrounds. Learn more at (704) 377-4187 or www.artsplus.org.

DEDICATION

For Sherri and our family.

For my sister Robyn, whom I dearly miss.

For the artists who make music

and the audiences that embrace it.

For the business partners, corporate clients,

club patrons, brides, mothers and everyone

else who helped me bring the harmony to life.

For the music that brings us together

if we hear it with open hearts.

"I LOVE MUSIC" | THE O'JAYS

I love music

any kind of music

I love music

just as long as it's groovin

makes me laugh, makes me smile

I love music

sweet sweet music

all the joy that it's bringin

TABLE OF CONTENTS

1

It Began With A Piano

2

The Business Of Music

3

A Dream Comes True

4

All That Jazz

5

A Lifetime Of Stories

6

My Friend Jay

7

Repairing The World

8

We Are Family

Larry, sister Robyn and their mother Sydelle, 1957. A few dates with photos are best guesses.

PROLOGUE

This is for our grandchildren, Sutton, Mac and Sam (and hopefully more to come), because I want them to understand what music has meant in their Pop's life. It's for Sherri, our three sons, Adam, Harrison and Reid, and their families, because we need to preserve the moments that brought us so much joy. It's for Uncle Jack, Uncle Lou, Sam Oberman (my Poppy), family friend Karl Boxer and my old piano teacher, Ziggy Hurwitz, because they showed me the way.

This gathering of my life's stories and memories is for everyone who joined me on the journey – the guys and gals in my bands, business partners, families that allowed me to brighten their Bar Mitzvahs and weddings, little-known musicians and singers who entertained us with their promise, and superstars who dazzled us with their artistry. That includes James Taylor. I must tell you about the time he and I went searching for a harmonica before his Charlotte gig.

Larry, playing the piano at his Bar Mitzvah, Charlotte, 1964.

Above all, I'm putting all this on paper for every music-lover who joined me on this ride. Your applause, your dancing in the aisles, your singing the songs out loud, all are part of the soundtrack of my life. To everyone who ever ran into me at a concert or club and said, "Tell me that story about...," here you go.

For years, I've wanted to save these remembrances. Time flies. If you haven't started on your story, get busy. It took some inspiration to get me going. Our middle son, Harrison, and his wife, Julia Gray, blessed us with a third grandchild. Samuel Harrison Farber Jr. was born on Jan. 24, 2021. I turned 70 on May 18, 2021. These are the sort of milestones that get you thinking about your life. When I'm not around, who's going to tell Sam and his cousins about the night Aretha Franklin came to perform after the death of Whitney Houston and paid tribute to her honorary niece on stage?

So here's my story, how a kid from Charlotte grew up to become a piano player, agent, manager, beach music and jazz club owner, co-founder of a music booking agency, and creator of *Music With Friends*, a concert series that brings music's biggest names to smaller venues. I'll tell you about the bands I played in going back to when I was 12, and our crazy gigs. One was a cattle auction. I'll take you to the unsung side of music and how I tried to follow my teacher Mr. Hurwitz's advice: Play music for fun, master the business to support your family. I'll share stories of the artists I've been lucky to encounter – Aretha, Willie Nelson, The Eagles' Glenn Frey, Tony Bennett, Darius Rucker, Earth, Wind & Fire, Gladys Knight and many more. I'll tell you about the night Jackson Browne invited Maurice Wil-

The Farber and Saunders families on vacation, Wild Dunes, Isle of Palms, S.C., summer 2021.

liams to the stage to sing the classic that my friend Maurice wrote, "Stay." I can hear you singing to yourself, *"Stay, ah, just a little bit longer."* I savored every experience, admired every artist. Even the Godfather of Soul, James Brown, when he declared "cash only" or he wasn't taking the stage.

I've never stopped saying to myself, "I can't believe I'm backstage with…"

I've been blessed to use my music experience to support my faith home, Temple Beth El, and other causes. You need a gala organized and band booked? I'm your man. By sharing that part of my story, I hope it inspires you to use your gifts to help neighbors in need.

I also want to introduce you to the loved ones who shaped and encouraged me: My parents, Charles and Syd, and my sisters, Enid and Robyn. Enid is a gifted photographer in New York. We lost Robyn to a drunk driver in 1993, the day before her 40th birthday. I wish she could be here to read about her older brother. You'll read more about her later in the book. I count Jay Thomas among my loved ones. The former Charlotte radio deejay and actor was 69 when cancer took him in 2017. Such adventures we shared, as you'll read.

Besides memories and smiles, I hope you take one more thing from my story: The power of music to bring us together. Black, white, young, old, wherever you come from, whatever your station in life, we can all embrace the harmony. It doesn't matter if it's Bonnie Raitt or Beyonce, Tony Bennett or The Temptations (am I dating myself?). What matters is that music can be our common denominator.

How do I know? I've spent a lifetime watching audiences cheer as one.

I engaged Ken Garfield to help with this project. He's a freelance writer/editor. You may know him from his years at *The Charlotte (N.C.) Observer*, where he covered religion and occasionally reviewed concerts, including the Grateful Dead at the Coliseum and George Strait at Charlotte Motor Speedway. He grew up listening to The Beatles. When he was 12, he performed Petula Clark's "Downtown" for his fifth-grade class. He had nerve. Ken may be the only person who ever walked out of a Rolling Stones concert. He'll save that for his memoir. Ken shares my passion for music and a belief in the power of telling our stories.

Andy Solomon proofed the manuscript and offered solid suggestions.

Many of the photos in this book were taken by Charlotte photographer Donna Bise. One of the best in the business, and a good friend, she has helped chronicle *Music With Friends*. The family and band photos come from The Larry Farber Collection. In other words, photos stashed in my phone and all over the house. My sister, Enid, a professional photographer, also contributed some of her great work. The Scout Guide Charlotte (www.charlotte.thescoutguide.com) was kind enough to share the photo of Adam and me at *Middle C Jazz Club*. It was taken by MB Productions. The Scout Guide highlights some of our best local businesses. Bobby Roebuck (www.shottotheheadphotography.com), a noted jazz photographer in Winston-Salem, shared photos from *Middle C Jazz Club*. Thanks, too, to Associated Press for use of its image of Jay Thomas with Dave Letterman.

The striking design and marriage of words and photos is the work of Christine Long, a former *Charlotte Observer* graphic artist now based in Arizona. I asked Christine to share some of her musical favorites. Talk about eclectic taste, she cited Depeche Mode, Whitney Houston, Beastie Boys, U2, Chicago, Queen, Guns N' Roses, Hall and Oates, INXS, Prince, Sheryl Crow, Keith Urban, The Chicks, Linkin Park and Pink. Now that's a music lover.

One last thing: I'm telling my story to the best of my recollection. A lot of this stuff happened long ago. Forgive me if I mess up a name or date. My memory isn't what it used to be.

The Farbers at home in Cotswold, 1961.

CHAPTER 1

IT BEGAN WITH A PIANO

Going back 60 years, loved ones, friends, bandmates, even famed pianist Peter Nero – all of them showed me the way. Life changes. The world turns upside down. Through it all, music has been my rock. The brotherhood of the bands, the privilege of serenading brides and grooms, the opportunity to manage clubs and introduce legends to passionate crowds, the honor of bringing harmony to this fractious world. I was seven or eight when that road opened before me.

I was born and raised in Charlotte. My dad, Charles, was a textile salesman, among other pursuits. My mom, Syd, was a buyer for Ivey's department store. She also at one time owned a boutique at Cotswold Mall called The Parasol. Mom was a natural salesperson, full of personality. Dad was quiet. Together, each in their own way, they encouraged me to follow my path. Growing up, there was always music. I listened to The Beatles and Rolling Stones, then got hooked on Motown and R&B. My parents listened to the standards, Sinatra, Bennett and the like. I remember our family friend Karl Boxer. He was a jazz pianist and opened a club years ago on Monroe Road, The Keyboard Lounge. As a teenager, I'd listen to him play. I could hear the coolness.

Mom's side of the family helped nurture my passion. I remember visiting my Uncle Jack Oberman in Philadelphia when I was a child. He had his own big band orchestra. He'd put me on his lap and play the piano. The music coming from his fingers was magic to me. His daughter (my cousin), Davida Oberman, grew up to play violin for Elvis, Wayne Newton and Doc Severinsen. With her long, red hair and sequined outfits, her showmanship captivated me. Davida was in her 60s when we lost her to cancer. Another uncle, Lou Oberman, went off to Hollywood to become a professional dancer. My mother's father, Sam Oberman, was rarely without his ukulele. He could only play a couple of songs. But how his eyes lit up when he played them. He was my Poppy. Now I'm a Poppy, sharing my life in music with my three grandchildren. When I was 10 years old, I went to my teacher Ziggy Hurwitz's studio in Dilworth for a 30-minute lesson. I'd play for 10 minutes and we'd talk for 20. He'd tell me to play music for the fun of it and, if you decide to go into the music business when you grow up, do it to support your family. Advice taken.

I have my good friend growing up, Craig Madans, to thank as well. One day we were at his house in the Cotswold neighborhood playing basketball when we took a break and went inside. There it was, the family's baby grand piano. Wow! I went home and convinced my parents to buy me my first piano, a Wurlitzer upright. It looked great in the living room of our Cotswold home. I started taking lessons with Mr. Hurwitz. I learned my first song on that pi-

Larry and Peter Nero, 1965.

ano with my friend Earl Dawkins on drums, "When the Saints Go Marching In." We were 11 or 12. It was the first time I experienced being in a band, everyone in sync, playing their part. The feeling was the fuel that propelled me.

At McClintock Junior High and Myers Park High, I played violin in the orchestra. I loved being part of something bigger than myself, school violinist by day, keyboardist for bands by nights and weekends. More inspiration: Famed pianist Peter Nero came to town for a show at Ovens Auditorium, then showed up at our house for the post-concert party. That new piano of ours? He autographed it for me: "Practice, dammit, practice." I could never bring myself to sell that piano. My son, Adam, has it. It's waiting for one of his children to learn to play it.

Nancy And The Persuasions.

The stuff you remember, and the moments that shape you.

At a talent show at McClintock Junior High, I performed "The Girl From Ipanema" on the piano. I was so nervous. A classmate, Debbie Byers, sang the same Latin-infused classic. We were both named winners. Years later, we wound up in the same bands, Debbie singing lead, me on keyboards. Sadly, Debbie Hartsell Byers passed away during the writing of this book. She was 70 years old. Her obituary recalled our performing together in R&B and beach music bands way back when. She'll forever be in my memory bank.

I was 12 years old when a bunch of us kids formed our first real band in 1963, The Nightcaps. My next-door neighbor, Steven Rousso, played guitar. Mike Citron was on drums. I was on keyboards.

The Rivieras.

Darned if I remember the bass player. Sorry, pal. I do remember our first gig: A Bar Mitzvah at Temple Israel, then on East Morehead Street. We made $20. Five bucks apiece. It was more than enough.

Over 44 years, I played in 20 bands give or take. The first professional one, Nancy And The Persuasions, practiced at my friend Otis Crowder's house. I was still a teenager. Nancy Barton sang vocals. Our high school band, The Rivieras, featured brothers Nat and Bobby Speir. Those guys could play. I never went to my own prom. We were too busy playing other people's proms. Our band at UNC-Chapel Hill, Main Street, included childhood pal Earl Dawkins on drums and Greg Cagle on bass and guitar. Greg, a banker by trade, and I played together 50 years. To this day, I can call him and ask "Remember what happened that night at so-and-so?" He will recount the story. One involved the time I was at UNC-Chapel Hill and had to hitchhike to Myrtle Beach for a gig. I got a ride to Pittsboro. That's where five coeds picked me up and drove me to the beach and back. We listened to The Temptations and Four Tops on the way. I wound up dating one of the coeds, Caroline Krisulewicz, during college. I told you, music and memories.

From junior high until long after I got into the music business as an agent and promoter, we performed at clubs (remember The Cellar on East Morehead?), Bar Mitzvahs, proms, weddings, resorts, charity balls, one cattle auction (more in a bit) and too many frat parties to count. "So that's what goes on at frat parties?!" I'd say to myself on the late-night ride home. At the Park Center on North Kings Drive (since renamed the Grady Cole Center), our high school band, The Rivieras, opened for The Four Tops, The Temptations, The Drifters, Smokey Robinson & The Miracles and others. Three or four acts would be on the bill, building up to these Motown acts that captivated us with their harmonies and choreography. The Park Center was an indelible part of life for a Charlotte-area kid growing up in the 1960s. For a $5 ticket at the door – $3 in advance – you could see the greatest that music had to offer. Google Little Anthony & The Imperials doing "Hurt So Bad." Is that not awesome? At The Embers Club in Raleigh and Atlantic Beach, we opened for Archie Bell & The Drells. Remember "Tighten Up?"

One of my bands, Eve, didn't last long. It was during my hippie phase. We played Jethro Tull and Led Zeppelin.

CHAPTER 1

Our bands averaged 30 gigs a year. That first one, the Bar Mitzvah, paid us $5 each. I'll never forget. When a few members of The Rivieras played Thursday nights at Paul's Lounge on South Boulevard, I took home $50. By the time we played the Marriott at Trade and Tryon on New Year's Eve 2000 – the new millennial – our band, Now 'n Then, made $10,000. My last gig, with Limited Edition, was May 19, 2017, at Quail Hollow Club. I need to tell you about that one.

There were so many bandmates who became soulmates. You probably know some of them: Greg Cagle, Earl Dawkins, Otis Crowder, Nat and Bobby Speir, Sammy Schiffman, Portia Vaughn, Bobby Aycock, Robyn Springer, Tina Fortunato, Joe Miers and Steve Mc-Guirt. Remember Debbie Byers? From that junior high talent show, where we each won with our versions of "Girl From Ipanema," we grew up to become bandmates and friends. I mourn her passing.

Every one of these folks, and all the others we shared the stage with, agree that it's not just the music we hold onto. It's the relationships, and the stories.

Our bands typically played gigs within a two- or three-hour drive from Charlotte. We'd pull a U-Haul trailer loaded with equipment, prepared to get lost in the days before GPS. You try finding a VFW hall in some small Southern town with just a map. I was usually the designated driver, for obvious reasons. Here was the coolest thing: When we played a frat party in Atlanta or Athens, Ga., we knew where to stop on the long ride home: That diner in Commerce, Ga. Who remembers the name, if it had one? All that mattered is it was open 24 hours. You'd stumble inside to encounter a diner full of other musicians driving home from their gigs. Driving home from Chapel Hill, you stopped at the Blue Mist in Asheboro, whose sign bragged "We Doze But We Never Close." I'd order a chef salad or barbecue. We'd finish the drive home in the dead of night, AM radio and our cassettes providing the soundtrack until we pulled in at dawn.

Playing weddings was a privilege or, at the very least, a surprise. At one, a lovely no-alcohol celebration on a family farm in Greensboro, the first dance went not to the bride and groom but to the bride's grandparents. They danced to "You Are the Sunshine of My Life." At a wedding party in Charlotte, we nailed "Butterfly Kisses" (remember, daddy's thankful for his little girl's butterfly kisses?) for the first dance. Only that wasn't the song they asked us to play for the first dance. Our bad. During the break, we learned the right song and came back and did "Wind Beneath My Wings." You never knew what you'd get at a wedding. At one in Charlotte, the father of the bride rose to give his toast and praise his favorite daughter. Only, drink in hand, it was his other daughter he praised. We all sat there – band, guests, wait staff, bride and groom most of all – dumbfounded. Somewhere in eastern North Carolina, one of the guests wanted to get up and perform – Tennessee Ernie Ford. We duct-taped a microphone to a broomstick so he could sing his signature "Sixteen Tons." At still another in Bluefield, W. Va., a guest died on the dance floor. The wedding halted, we drove home.

Once – and only once – in Georgia, we played for a cattle auction. Each time a cow was auctioned off, we played an appropriate song, including the theme from the TV show "Dallas." When three calves were sold, we played the Commodores hit, "Three Times A Lady."

Now that you've gotten the idea, I saved the wackiest for last.

It was May 2017. I was 66 years old. Time for the old(er) man to exit stage left after one last show, a fancy party at Quail Hollow Club for a member-guest golf tournament. Our 10-piece band, Limited Edition, featured three singers. We did everything from Motown to Bruno Mars. We played a great first set. We took the stage for the second set and no one was there. Were we that bad? Turned out everyone had jumped into golf carts and raced over to the 50th birthday party for a local businessman whose home was on the golf course. The backyard entertainment for that party? Justin Timberlake.

From the beginning, I tried to follow Mr. Hurwitz's advice. It wasn't hard. Music is fun whether you're serenading cows or driving home on I-85, cracking up over what just took place at that frat party you played. I also believe that starting my journey on stage made me a better promoter, agent and club owner. I love performers. I know what they need to be successful, whether it's the preshow buffet or a fair price for their services. Music. It's all a blast, whether you're opening a jazz club in uptown Charlotte or introducing Sheryl Crow to the *Music With Friends* crowd. I hope that comes through as I tell the rest of my story.

Sixty years. Rarely does an old song come on the radio that doesn't take me back. I covered that one at a thousand gigs. That's the one we played for the bride and groom's first dance. That's the one I learned to play on the piano my parents bought me when I was a kid all those years ago.

Party on the Moon.

CHAPTER 2
THE BUSINESS OF MUSIC

I love music. I also love the business of music. I wasn't satisfied just to be the keyboard player in the band that got everyone up and dancing at a wedding or frat party. I wanted to be the guy who marketed the band, booked the date, handled the logistics, closed the deal, then came home with the check or, as my bandmates preferred, cash. Someone had to stay clear-headed (and sober) enough to do it.

It's how I'm wired. During the pandemic, Sherri and I took a quick getaway to Wild Dunes, S.C. in the Isle of Palms, S.C. I enjoyed the R&R at the resort not far from Charleston. But I couldn't stop thinking to myself, "How can we revive *Music With Friends* in Charleston?" More on that venture, the joy of my life, in the next chapter. My brain is always working overtime. My phone is always ringing. My calling is to bring music and joy to people. I'm not afraid of trying or failing. I once joined with some partners to promote an outdoor concert featuring Three Doors Down at the minor-league baseball stadium in Charleston. We didn't have enough rain insurance. It rained. We took

Alive After Five, uptown Charlotte, 2018.

a bath. But I could live with that. We gave it a shot.

It's the art of the deal, a dozen a day percolating at times, hammering out the details, building relationships that last a lifetime, then seeing and hearing it all come alive when that first note is played. Rough estimate, ballpark, I figure I booked 100,000 dates in my career.

Early on, I booked bands for The Town Pump on Hay Street in Fayetteville. What a versatile place. It doubled as a dance club and

Black & Blue Experience.

strip club. Its nickname was The Town Dump. When I'd visit, I'd wonder what my parents thought about my career choice, this over being a lawyer. The first band I managed, Times Square, played there.
Earl Dawkins was on drums – my childhood friend who played with
me when I learned my first song on the piano, "When the Saints Go
Marching In." The bands at The Town Pump played when the dancers
were on break. It's not up there with booking the Dave Matthews

Band for a debutante ball at Myers Park Country Club. But you know what? I made a lifelong friend, a great guy, Joey Monseur, who owned The Town Dump. I mean The Town Pump.

Music, deals, friends and memories.

My parents weren't the only ones, Jewish or otherwise, who yearned for their child to be a doctor, lawyer or accountant. I was a good student at UNC-Chapel Hill. I even got wait-listed at the law school after I graduated. But then came the Spring of 1972 when our Tar Heels basketball team made the Final Four in Los Angeles. We started batting around some ideas at the Tau Epsilon Phi fraternity house. I was fraternity president. LA's not that far, right? That's how my first big deal came to pass: I arranged for two United airplanes to fly from Chicago to the Raleigh-Durham airport, pick up two planeloads of students – 140 in all – and fly them to the game. Each student paid $73 roundtrip. I made $4 per ticket. With the $560 in profit, I took two frat brothers and my girlfriend to LA. It was all worth it, even if the Tar Heels didn't win. UCLA, with Bill Walton, did.

For that one weekend, Larry The Ordinary Student was Larry The Dealmaker. I could see the path ahead. I graduated from UNC-Chapel Hill on Sunday, May 13, 1973. On Monday, I reported to work on the eighth floor of the Cameron Brown Building on South McDowell Street. My job? An agent with the booking agency Hit Attractions, working for Ted Hall. We lost him in 2019. I owe so much to Ted. I owe so much as well to Harvey Grasty, another booking agent at Hit Attractions. He passed away in 2021. He was 78. What a lovely man. Such fun we shared. My pay that first year at Hit Attractions? I earned

Now 'n Then.

$7,500. My commissions for booking bands starting out was as low as $30 a gig. Back then, that was fine with me. (It did go up thankfully.) More than pay, I earned a love of the business, and lifelong connections with Ted and Harvey among others.

I was off and running. I was performing in bands. I was managing other bands. I opened my first club, The Boardwalk, on Monroe Road. Beach music legends General Johnson and Chairmen of the Board ("Carolina Girls") was the first band to play there. Turns out there was another beach music club nearby, The Treehouse. We were splitting the business so I made a deal with them. For $15,000, I'll close. Deal done. The Boardwalk will always hold a place in my heart. It's where I met a funny local deejay, Jay Thomas, at closing time. He was working at Big WAYS Radio at the time, killing it in the ratings. There's a great story there that I'll share later. Jay became a TV (remember "Murphy Brown?") and film star ("Mr. Holland's Opus"). We became lifelong friends. He was 69 when cancer took him in 2017.

My job at Hit Attractions took me to frat and sorority houses across the Southeast, booking bands for their parties. I'd try to meet in a neutral location like the library, always less nasty than the living room of a frat house. I'd book a band, then attend the party, typically standing by the sound board to make sure everything went smoothly. Often I'd be joined by sorority girls who were waiting for the band to finish. That's all I need to say about that. Many nights the party ended with The Isley Brothers' classic "Shout!"

A bonus of the job: I'd book a band for a frat party. Then years later, I'd book a band for the wedding of some kid I met at the party. Then I'd book a band for his kids' weddings.

I was born to do this. My normal speed, even today, is 150 mph. I get along well with most everyone. Being a musician helps me appreciate what bands need to be successful.

I worked for Hit Attractions from 1973-86. They were some of the best years of my life. It's where I got my foothold in the business. But I'm the restless type, always wondering what's next. That "next" took root at Grossinger's, the iconic and long closed Jewish resort in the Catskills Mountains north of New York City. There, at a convention of people who ran college student unions and booked bands, I sat down with Dennis Huber and Steve Thomas. They were competitors who ran the booking agency, EastCoast Entertainment, founded in 1976 and based at the time in Richmond, Va. I dreamed of being part of an agency that could hire the best agents and book the best bands across the largest region. We cut a deal. I joined forces with Steve and Dennis as a senior managing partner. We eventually recruited my friends John Roth from Hit Attractions and Ed Duncan from Fisher & Stallings Associates. Lee Moore was elevated to a partner. Ed was creative, loyal and had a great vision for the music business. Eventually Ted Hall closed Hit Attractions and joined us at ECE. John, Ed and I opened the Charlotte office on Cleveland Avenue in Dilworth. Everyone was great to work with. Dennis was a blessing to me. He embodied every quality I admired. He cared about the bands and music. There was no BS with him, just compassion. He died too soon from brain cancer in 1998.

At ECE, our vision was coming to life. At its peak (which is now), EastCoast Entertainment grew to include nearly 15 offices and some 50 agents bringing in $10 million a year in net commissions. That's more than $100 million in annual bookings. There are roughly 400 bands under our wing exclusively. These were some of the best and most familiar bands going, bands you probably danced to on some

EastCoast Entertainment partners with Steely Dan, 2009.

night somewhere. Early on, think of The Voltage Brothers, Fantastic Shakers, The Rivieras and The Catalinas. Mr. Potato Head was popular. Mr. Potato Head performed a decade ago at the wedding of my writing helper Ken Garfield's daughter. Ken says they were kind enough to learn Otis Redding's "That's How Strong My Love Is" for his first dance with Ellen a decade ago. The only screwup? Ken was so overcome with emotion he forgot his checkbook. At midnight, he had to drive back to the house to pay the band. Today, the hot bands you may be booking for your next party are Simply Irresistible, Atlanta Showstoppers, Sol Fusion and Black & Blue Experience. Ted Hall (a different Ted Hall from Hit Attractions) is the lead singer for Black & Blue. What a gem of a guy. I managed and booked that band for more than 40 years, unheard of in this line of work. Ted and I became as close as brothers. When he got married at one of those small chapels in Las Vegas, I flew out to join the wedding crowd, which totaled four of us. That included the bride and groom.

I once booked Kenny Mann and Liquid Pleasure for the Bar Mitzvah of a 13-year-old youngster, Sonny Gold, whose family I knew well. The party was at Mar-a-Lago (long before its owner was President of the United States). Bells and whistles included synchronized swimmers performing during cocktail hour around the pool. I got to play golf with one of the guests, Lee Trevino. That was another time I said to myself, "I love this job."

In the midst of writing this book, I was texting back and forth with the mother of a bride-to-be. Mom wanted to book Big Swing & the Ballroom Blasters for her daughter's wedding in New York. She was a delight to deal with. Katie Couric. More later.

Party On The Moon is probably the No. 1 wedding and corporate party band today. They've played for President Obama, sheiks and NFL stars. They get up to $35,000 for a Saturday night wedding within a few hours of their home in Atlanta, more if it's in, say, Jackson Hole, Wyoming. Confetti cannons are extra.

Want to have some fun? Check out ECE bands' videos at www.bookece.com. Don't miss Liquid Pleasure. Having President Obama sing your praises is cool.

Maybe here's where I need to address Band Booking 101.

The normal industry standards for gross commissions earned by the company range between 10 and 20 percent. Agents make a percentage of these commissions. I was proud to have introduced the concept of a draw vs. commission. This way an agent could earn a base salary (the draw) supplemented by a commission. This structure incentivizes an agent to do well. I also pushed for an ownership model that rewards a percentage of ownership plus your personal production. You book synchronized swimmers for a Bar Mitzvah, you deserve whatever you earn.

My ECE years – I officially retired from the company Dec. 31, 2019, though I'm nowhere near "retired" – were the most electric of my career. In addition to growing the company and booking acts, I managed bands on my own and pursued other ventures. Remember, trying and failing doesn't scare me.

I managed Maurice Williams & The Zodiacs, whose eternally great hit "Stay" got new life when it was featured in the classic film "Dirty Dancing." Maurice, a close friend who still lives in Charlotte, and I attended the wrap party on Lake Lure. The star of the movie was there. Patrick Swayze.

It didn't last long, but I put together a super group, Legends of Soul, featuring Maurice, Clifford Curry ("Double Shot Of My Baby's Love") and Archie Bell ("Tighten Up" with the Drells). When they performed, it was like being in beach music heaven.

When an Arab sheik needed a band for the opening of a luxury hotel in Addis Ababa, Ethiopia, I got them soul and funk legends Kool & the Gang ("Celebration").

I handled a lot of private events independent of ECE – birthday parties, Super Bowl bashes (including 2004 in Houston when the Panthers fell to New England), class reunions, corporate gatherings and the like. Ray Charles for then-First Union. B.J. Thomas ("Raindrops Keep Fallin' on My Head") for businessman Johnny Harris' birthday party at Sea Island, Ga. Jim Belushi and the Sacred Hearts Band for auto mogul Skipper Beck's party at his former home on the Quail Hollow golf course. I recall that the party celebrated Skipper getting to sell the uber-luxury car, Maybach. The party cost Skipper more than a few dollars. But he got to give Belushi a tour of his media room and wristwatch collection and wound up selling him a couple of cars.

Michael and Ann Tarwater were two of my best clients and friends. Ann has a flair for putting on a party. When Michael retired as head of Atrium Health, the party featured the Diana Ross character from the Broadway show "Motown: The Musical" plus Big Swing & the Ballroom Blasters. For a fundraiser, the Tarwaters had me bring in Philip Bailey, one of the founders of Earth, Wind & Fire.

The Supremes, Doobie Brothers, Chicago. I booked them all.

Ever attend one of those big block parties at Phillips Place during the Wells Fargo golf tournament? I booked the bands, stars like Huey Lewis and the News. Golf tournament concerts were great, especially when the likes of John Daly and Sergio Garcia got up to sing with the band. Once at Phillips Place, John Daly sang his go-to song, "Knockin' On Heaven's Door." It wasn't Dylan, but it wasn't bad for a hard-living golfer. At another golf party, Sergio Garcia performed "Mustang Sally." He was no Wilson Pickett, but he was good.

Ever party at Alive After Five, the uptown concert series launched in 1999? Ed Duncan, Paul Chanon and I created the event. Ed and I once booked a fast-rising country band from Atlanta for $800. Years later, I booked them for a concert for $1 million. The Zac Brown Band.

For $3,500, the debutantes who were "coming out" one year in the mid-1990s at Myers Park Country Club danced to the Dave Matthews Band. Live. I remember the social director grumbling about what the band requested in terms of dressing rooms, food and the like. I doubt she'd grumble now. Then again, I doubt Dave Matthews would play a debutante ball today for $3,500.

Back when they were just a popular bar band from South Carolina, I booked Hootie & the Blowfish for $1,000 to play local clubs. Darius Rucker, of course, has since turned into a country star. He still plays with his old rock band. I consider him a friend. He probably remembers the party where John Daly kissed him on his lips.

Humpy Wheeler was the ultimate P.T. Barnum when he ran Charlotte Motor Speedway. This was back in the days when race fans filled that mammoth venue and demanded more than cars going around and around. Humpy gave it to them, what he used to call a three-ring circus. One year, he reenacted the military invasion of Grenada. I booked pop culture celebrities to make appearances in the fancy Speedway suites and around the track, among them Leonard Nimoy (Spock) and Larry Hagman (J.R.). Leonard was a gentleman. I took him to several art galleries before his appearance at the Speedway. Larry was a charmer and a ham, 10-gallon cowboy hat and all. I remember we were stuck in traffic, trying to get to the Speedway, when Humpy arranged for a police escort. "Who the hell made that happen?" Larry asked me. "You're about to meet him," I answered.

My dream and determination at ECE was to get bigger and better.

Alive After Five rocks uptown, 2018.

We launched a speaker's bureau and a deejay division for those whose budget couldn't cover live music for their daughter's wedding. Comedy Zone merged with ECE, a deal that took 20 years. I became great friends with Comedy Zone's Brian Heffron.

In 2008, we joined forces with Daniel Entertainment, our main competitor in Charlotte. It was founded by former ECE agent Doug Daniel, who became ECE's president and CEO for a few years. Susan Criner in Houston was a friend who ran Gulf Coast Entertainment. We partnered on *Music With Friends* in Houston. In 2019, when the timing was right, that company merged with ECE. By that time, Susan came into the fold with her daughter, Annie Eifler. The special events division we started – a one-stop shop for all things weddings – seemed like a good idea at the time. Only the wedding planners didn't think so. Oh well. There's always another idea around the bend. Whatever the project, I heeded the lesson my Poppy, Sam Oberman, taught me. You remember him. He always had a ukulele in his hands, hie eyes always sparkling. He taught me the three F's: Be firm. Be friendly. Be fair.

There are so many people who joined me on this journey, whose friendship mean a lot to me. Whatever your business, life's most important lesson is that you don't do anything alone.

After I joined Dennis and Steve at ECE, we added Lee Moore, Ed Duncan and John Roth, mentioned earlier in this chapter. Remember, I tried to hire Ed out of college, but he opted for Fisher-Stallings initially. John Roth started with Ed at Fisher, left shortly after for Hit Attractions, then became part of this original six in 1986. Years later, we added Rick Stowe, John Wolfslayer and Steve Harry as partners, all promoted from agents. Our next round of partners included Mark Letson, Barry Herndon in the Raleigh office (he came up playing in the bands like me, Cream of Soul) and Doug Daniel. Doug started as an agent, left to open a competing agency, then Ed and I convinced him to come back again years later. He took early retirement in 2020. We also added partners Matthew Thomas, Chris McClure, who is like a son to me, and Kris Kaminski, who is part of the legacy. Her mom worked with us before passing away. Chris works in Charlotte and has been a huge part of *Music With Friends*. Ellie Schwartz runs the Asheville office. As mentioned, Brian Heffron, Annie Eifler and Susie Criner are the newest partners from our latest mergers. Toni Cline was with ECE from the start. Others at ECE who contributed to my and the company's success included my assistants Aliza Sherman, Colby Bell, Susan Branch, Sheldon Ingram, Hank Patterson and David Krusch.

In the early years at Hit Attractions, Dave Fisher and Harvey Grasty were mainstays. Karen Hall Broyhill was my first assistant.

ECE is still thriving. I have lots of friends there. We talk all the time. That agency is dear to my heart for another reason. The youngest of our three boys, Reid, is an agent there. A UNC-Chapel Hill graduate, his dreams and abilities – he's patient and organized unlike me – could have taken him anywhere. But he heard the music and listened to the stories his father shared over the years. Now he's in the music business. There's a Yiddish word that describes how I feel when someone tells me how great Reid is. *Naches*. Pride and joy.

It's been 35 years since I left Hit Attractions to go with EastCoast Entertainment. I still remember how daunting a decision that was, and what my wife, Sherri, asked me at the time.

"Are you sure you know what you're doing?"

A lifetime later, after all the music, deals, friendships and memories, having never gone a day without a job, having a son follow a similar path, I have an answer for Sherri.

"We did OK on that one."

Bonnie Raitt, 2011.

CHAPTER 3

A DREAM COMES TRUE

M usic *With Friends* is my dream come true.

All I ever wanted to do was bring joy to the world (with apologies to Three Dog Night) through music. My mission has been to help people put aside their cares while the band played, to help us find common ground with our neighbors. Whether it's beach music, the blues or rock, the genre doesn't matter. What matters is that the first note sounds and we smile. Maybe we get up and dance. Maybe this unity extends beyond one night of music.

Music With Friends is the embodiment of everything I believe music can be. I came to appreciate that the night we debuted our private music club. It was the Spring of 2007. McGlohon Theater at Spirit Square in uptown Charlotte was filled with 100 patrons, the first to join this new adventure. The theater shone with beauty and stained glass, recalling its roots as a Baptist church. Following a cocktail party, Michael McDonald took the stage. His hair had turned silver since his days with Steely Dan and, most famously, The Doobie Brothers.

But that voice remains distinctive, described by one writer as smooth, warm and buttery, soft and gritty all at once. He opened with "Takin' It to the Streets." The crowd was a mix of music lovers of all ages, though "mature" (50s and up) is a good word to describe them. No offense, friends. I'm one of you. At the first note, they moved to the rock classic and that opening lyric, "You don't know me but I'm your brother."

Music With Friends was off and running and it's never stopped, except, of course, for COVID-19. I remember looking out onto the crowd that first night and saying to myself, "This is cooler than I could ever have imagined."

Fourteen years and 40 (and counting) concerts later, it's still cool. Let me elaborate.

One day in 2006, Charlotte lawyer Jeff Davis, a longtime friend of mine, called and invited me to lunch. That's where he sprang the idea, born from his love of the McGlohon Theater. Go once and you'll love it, too. He wanted to join me in promoting shows there. I suggested we revise the idea: Let's start a private music club and recruit friends, neighbors and others to attend shows at McGlohon. We'll put on several concerts a year (we eventually settled on three a year). The crowd will be small. The hall is intimate so the patrons and artist can look each other in the eye. Many have been legends with whom we grew up, still active when they joined us, no nostalgia tours here. Think of Aretha Franklin, Bonnie Raitt and Willie Nelson. The acoustics are pristine so every note will sound crystal clear. The evening will begin with a cocktail hour, no chicken wings, think shrimp, prime rib and top-shelf drinks. This will be so unique that patrons will happily pay a

Poster celebrating 10 years of Music With Friends, 2017.

one-time joining fee plus an annual fee for three shows each year. We'll even send around the names of available artists in our price range and find out who patrons want to hear. (As of late, they're warming up to

Gladys Knight, 2007.

Jackson Browne and Maurice Williams, 2008.

country music, broadening the genres we can offer.)

It sounded a little crazy. But for Baby Boomers and an older crowd that has grown tired of crowded arenas, drunken fans, traffic jams, parking snafus, long concession lines and seats a mile from the stage, an intimate music club sounds enticing. Plus, "crazy" ideas are right up my alley. As I told *Business North Carolina* magazine for a profile they wrote of me, "If I'm not doing something different, a little bit of me is dying."

We figured we needed 400 members to make it work financially. Currently we have 520 members even amid these uncertain times. The current cost to belong includes a one-time joining fee of $550 that obligates you to buy tickets to three shows a year at a cost of $1,650 a year. Patrons get the same seats for each concert. In 2021, the shows go on, though in a new venue due to renovations at Spirit Square. We'll be at the Sarah Belk Gambrell Center at Queens University of Charlotte. Because the pandemic cost us all but one show in 2020, we'll do two late in 2021 to mark our 15th anniversary: Pat Benatar and her husband and musical partner Neil Giraldo on October 14 and Kenny Loggins on November 16. Think "Hit Me With Your Best Shot" and "Footloose."

Let's talk business first.

We knew artists would be drawn to the intimacy of the *Music With Friends* experience. After her show in 2011, Bonnie Raitt (what a delight she was to work with) told us, "I can't believe I am getting paid to play for this incredible crowd in this beautiful venue." The atmosphere lends itself to artists creating a relationship with the audience and sharing personal stories and banter. At one point, Glenn Frey, who co-founded The Eagles, stopped to grab a tissue before closing his show in 2012 with "Take it to the Limit." This is as close as any of us will get to sitting in a legend's living room, sharing music and conversation. As Glenn put it, you can feel the band breathe, feel the music. We lost a genius when he passed away in 2016 at age 67.

The challenge was to convince folks that the experience is worth their time and money. We networked with everyone we knew. We hosted small gatherings to sell the experience. Folks with influence led the way. For example, auto executive Skipper Beck was our first patron. He bought 10 front-row seats. Tragically, Skipper was killed in a small

Willie Nelson, 2013.

plane crash in 2009. Former Carolina Panthers coach John Fox and his wife, Robin, bought in. Others followed. Most people in the demographic we were pinpointing have discretionary income. They came to appreciate that investing in *Music With Friends* is a wise move.

We took care with every aspect. We avoid shows in summer and December when many people are out of town or otherwise engaged. We hold them on weekdays rather than weekends when people are also away or busy. A cocktail reception kicks off the evening at 6 p.m. The 90-minute shows begin at 7:30 p.m. so people can get home at a reasonable hour. We avoid the dead of winter to avoid weather snafus. When we noticed that concert-goers were in no rush to leave after the show, we began hosting post-show cocktail parties at restaurants so everyone can linger and talk about what they had just seen and heard.

The reviews have been consistently great. Patrons love the blend of "exclusivity" and intimacy and the chance to be together. One gentleman said it's the best three dates he has each year with his wife. Getting to network with the city's movers and shakers is a bonus.

If you've gotten this far in the book, you know me. Why couldn't we expand *Music With Friends* to cities all across the country? We created the second *Music With Friends* in Charleston, S.C., in 2010. Diana Ross was our first artist. But the famed Dock Street Theater, while beautiful, was too small to make the economics work. Vince Gill closed the show for good on the night President Trump was elected in 2016. We tried Nashville, Tenn. Diana Ross opened the show there, too, this time at the new CMA Theater at the Country Music Hall of Fame. But the costs in Music City USA were too high. Country mu-

Sheryl Crow, 2010.

sic's Jennifer Nettles performed the final show in Nashville. Thanks to John Huie from Creative Arts Agency, who helped me get started in Nashville. The show goes on in Houston at The George Theater in the vibrant Galleria District. We're still figuring out whether Houston is economically viable. Like everywhere else, it's artistically viable.

At one point, we looked at affluent Greenwich, Conn. I get calls all the time from entrepreneurs in other cities. John Wayne's daughter called. She was thinking about bringing *Music With Friends* to Orange County, California. We "franchised" *Music With Friends* to Newark, N.J., at the Victoria Theater at the New Jersey Performing Arts Center and to Washington, D.C. at the Sidney Harman Hall in the popular Penn Quarter. The key in each locale is having a city with deep business and social connections. The brand is gaining strength.

Little in the music business remains the same. In 2009, I bought out Jeff Davis' share. He knew he needed to focus on his law career. I remain grateful for his friendship, partnership and inviting me to lunch to unveil the original idea. I recruited some great and prominent people to join the ownership group: Johnny Harris, Steve Cummings, David Rudolf, Russ Krueger and Clay Boardman. Then it became Clay and me. Now, it's just me. What's the future of *Music With Friends*? More legends, more music, perhaps in more cities. I was 56 when Michael McDonald started it all. I'm 70 now. Maybe I'll let the Farber boys in on the fun.

I started with the business side of the story. I've got to end with the music. I'm still starstruck in front of the artists who join us at *Music With Friends*. It's given me a chance to be in the presence of those who are part of the great American soundtrack.

Tony Bennett came that first year, 2007. In my excitement, I sometimes refer to him as "Friggin' Tony Bennett" such is his greatness. We put him up at The Dunhill Hotel across from Spirit Square. I escorted him across the street for sound check, which lasted four minutes.

Tony Bennett, 2007.

That's all he needed to pronounce that the acoustics were great. "I left my heart in San Francisco…" and he was done.

A postscript about Tony. He and Lady Gaga shared the stage at Radio Music City Hall in New York for what turned out to be his last public performance. Tony, 95 at this writing, suffers from Alzheimer's disease. You couldn't tell it from the final gift he left us – a video of

Lady Gaga and him performing "I Get A Kick Out of You." Watch it. It seems bathed in a golden hue. Listen to it. The greatest jazz singer of them all sounds like a neatly poured martini, smooth and clean. The greatest pop star of the day sounds as enchanting as Ella. Together, they span the generations, their voices part of American music.

Another legend performed in 2007, Gladys Knight (sans Pips). She is so gracious. She was playing on a tennis team in Asheville at the time. She brought the entire team to the show.

I touched on it in the prologue, but it remains one of my favorite stories. When Jackson Browne came to perform in 2008, I mentioned to him that Maurice Williams, the artist who wrote "Stay," lives in Charlotte. Jackson's version of "Stay" had become a hit. He called Maurice and said, "How quickly can you get here?" A little history: Maurice was 15 when he wrote the song in 1953, inspired by his effort to convince his date not to go home. Maurice Williams and the Zodiacs recorded it in 1960. Others to record it were The Hollies, The Four Seasons and, of course, Jackson Browne. That evening in 2008, *Music With Friends* featured Jackson and Maurice performing a duet of the shortest song (one minutes 36 seconds) ever to hit No. 1 on the American charts. I remember Jackson introducing Maurice to the band as if he was a musical God. He is.

I'm no matchmaker but I remember an appearance by Sheryl Crow in 2010. In the audience was golfer Fred Couples, in town for the Quail Hollow golf championship. I believe Crow and Couples were both single at the time. That might explain why Couples asked me to introduce him to Sheryl. They posed for a picture together.

Music With Friends team.

That's all I know.

So many people have played a part in helping make *Music With Friends* what it is today. First I must thank the hundreds of Charlotte music lovers who became a "friend." Their enthusiasm for the music and experience has made this a success. Jeff Davis is my friend and former partner who helped get this rolling. My EastCoast Entertainment partner Chris McClure has produced all the shows. Another ECE partner, Mark Letson, helped book most of the acts. Missy Crews Howard helped get all this off the ground. Leslie Ka-

Earth, Wind & Fire, 2011.

plan Schlernitzauer and Bruce Schlernitzauer of Porcupine Provi-
sions have handled the catering from day one. The food, beverage
and ambience is a huge part of our brand. Al Smith of Paragon
Productions has handled the sound and backline production. Missy
Hoopingarner was our bookkeeper. For a decade, Becky Mitchener
handled marketing and sales. Becky couldn't have done it without
Ann Linde. Tonda Rifkin is our current sales and marketing ace.
My friend, Cantey Hare, in Charleston has been a great supporter.
So has Tom Gabbard, longtime President and CEO of Blumenthal
Performing Arts. To all these friends and partners, and to everyone
else who has been part of the *Music With Friends* story, my deepest
thanks.

Michael McDonald with Adam, wife Sarah and Larry, 2007.

There will be more stories, including the circumstances that led to Aretha's unforgettable night on the *Music With Friends* stage. But I want to close this chapter by going back to the beginning.

Michael McDonald arrived in town for that first show in 2007. Partner Jeff Davis and I took him and his daughter to dinner at Lavecchia's Seafood Grille, then a popular uptown spot. That's where Michael told me about his love of beach music, the Carolinas-rich version, more like The Embers than The Beach Boys. Who knew? The next day – the day of the show – *Music With Friends* faced its first test. Michael had a dental issue. When my heart stopped thumping, we found a dentist to work him in at the last minute. That evening as I paced from one end of Spirit Square to the other, waiting to see if this daring new venture would crash or soar, I heard music coming from Michael's dressing room. He was warming up on a portable keyboard, the voice of a Rock and Roll Hall of Famer that would soon sing for us all.

"Holy s---," I remember saying to myself.

Here's everyone who has played *Music With Friends* in Charlotte. Scan the names. Recall their hits. Want to become part of *Music With Friends* and/or keep up with what's going on? Visit us at www.musicwithfriends.com.

THE LINEUP

2007
Michael McDonald
Gladys Knight
Tony Bennett

2008
George Benson/Al Jarreau
Boz Scaggs
Jackson Browne

2009
Smokey Robinson
Steely Dan
Loggins and Messina

2010
Sheryl Crow
Daryl Hall & John Oates
Crosby, Stills & Nash

2011
Diana Ross
Earth, Wind & Fire
Bonnie Raitt

2012
Aretha Franklin
Darius Rucker
Glenn Frey

2013
Doobie Brothers
Willie Nelson
Steve Miller

2014
Heart
Foreigner
Michael Bolton

2015
Steve Winwood
Chicago
Joe Walsh

2016
Temptations/Four Tops
Steely Dan
America/Christopher Cross

2017
Norah Jones
Commodores

2018
Styx
ZZ Top
Alison Krauss
Three Dog Night

2019
Lyle Lovett
Gladys Knight
Boz Scaggs

2020
Chris Botti

2021
Pat Benatar/Neil Giraldo
Kenny Loggins

Adam and Larry, Middle C Jazz Club, Charlotte.

CHAPTER 4

ALL THAT JAZZ

I f *Music With Friends* was my dream come true, *Middle C Jazz Club* is my legacy. It is an ode to the music my parents played years ago, Ella and Frank, Count Basie and the Duke, those old 78s and 45s bringing a coolness to our Cotswold home.

Jazz lived way back then, especially in the Farber home. I'm working to make sure jazz lives today and tomorrow. Jazz, unfortunately, doesn't fill arenas like pop and rock. For all their talent, the names of saxophonist Ronnie Laws nationally and vocalist Maria Howell and pianist/composer Noel Freidline regionally don't make the cash registers turn like Taylor Swift or Bruce Springsteen. It's hard to sell records without MTV playing you 24/7, and without your stars dominating social media. Jazz is too sophisticated for all that stuff anyway. Give us an intimate club with the lights turned low. Serve up a martini. Put a soloist or quartet on stage to improvise in front of a couple of hundred pure fans and you're talking jazz. Welcome to *Middle C.*

The idea of a first-class jazz club in Charlotte percolated in my head for two decades. I wanted a place where artists, often underpaid and underappreciated, could own the spotlight. Where jazz lovers could hear their music not just at a one-off festival but at a club open four to five nights a week. Where the acoustics are clear and the crowds come to listen, not talk (a pet peeve). Where years from now, long after I am gone, *Middle C* will have grown in stature to become one of those enduring places that helps define our city. I've been around the music business long enough to know that a jazz club wasn't going to make me rich. But I believed that helping keep this genre alive in my hometown would be reward enough.

Jazz has had an uphill climb in Charlotte. The last regular club in town – Jonathan's Jazz Cellar – operated from 1984 to 1994 at Seventh and Tryon streets. Thanks to the Gellman family for keeping that club going. I loved dropping by The Double Door Inn on Independence Boulevard, closed now, which used to include jazz occasionally in its lineup. There have been some great jazz festivals and special jazz events. The Bechtler Museum of Modern Art uptown draws some nice crowds for its one-Friday-a-month jazz gatherings. The nonprofit JazzArts Charlotte (www.thejazzarts.org) takes jazz into all corners of the community.

But jazz deserves its own home.

Working with my son, Adam, who's a successful commercial real estate agent and who loves music, we started scouting potential properties. We wanted to stand out, so we avoided the tangle and traffic around the Epicentre and Fifth Street bars. We settled on brand-new, ground-floor space at 300 S. Brevard St., near the Convention Center, Spectrum Center and NASCAR Hall of Fame. We're close to the

Jazz pianist Lovell Bradford, Middle C, 2021.

light rail and connected to a parking deck. We visited jazz clubs in other cities to see what makes them thrive. We decided not to do a "franchise" deal in which we take the name of a nationally known club like the Blue Note in New York's Greenwich Village. We wanted this to belong solely to Charlotte. How committed were we? We raised $1¼ million from 20 or so investors, many of them friends and associates. Some had me book their children's Bar Mitzvah and wedding bands. We are grateful to each one of them. To prove how serious we were, we paid two years rent in advance.

We transformed the space – concrete and blank walls – into the quintessential jazz club. A slightly elevated stage. Low ceiling. Dark curtains. Great sight lines. For $25,000 I bought a used seven-foot Yamaha grand piano I found on sale in the Midwest. If all else fails, I assured my family, at least we'd have another grand piano for the house. We decorated the walls with posters of jazz greats like Billie Holiday and Tony Bennett. We hung posters celebrating (and cross-promoting) *Music With Friends*. Some of the photos on the wall were taken by my sister Enid, a gifted music photographer in New York. For drinks and food – a dozen or so small plates and sharables – we partner with The Public House, a spacious restaurant/bar across the hallway from Middle C. Former WBTV sports anchor Delano Little is part of the ownership group.

You want a challenge? Open a club and deal with permits, signage, the sound system, lighting, glassware, food and beverage, carpet, artwork, social media, sales and merchandise. You need to book acts and private events, create a first-class experience for the artists, handle personnel and payroll and, oh yes, deal with a pandemic that wound up shutting us down for 2½ months. One of my most emotional moments at *Middle C* came the night we returned from COVID-19. Those first notes from the bass and keyboards sounded and I said to myself, "I'm hearing live music again."

From the start, our plan was to put on four to five shows a week, 300 shows a year with seating for 200.

Opening Night. November 2, 2019. Oops. That was the night of *Chai On Laughter*, a fund-raiser for my faith home, Temple Beth El, that I helped organize. The star of the show was comedian Paul Reiser ("Mad About You"). He did a wonderful 75 minutes. How was I going to be at two places? Watch me. Around 9 p.m., I asked Paul, "You want

Middle C Jazz Club, 2021.

to go hear some good music?" Together, we tiptoed out of the gala at Spirit Square and into *Middle C*, where vocalist Maria Howell and pianist/band leader Noel Freidline were playing to a full house.

To this day, my friend Maria says that performing on opening night in front of Paul Reiser is one of her *Middle C* highlights.

My son Adam says Opening Night was his personal highlight, too. After two-plus years of work, all the stress melted away in the music. For him, for all of us, Opening Night was a healing experience.

Opening Night was special for my wife, Sherri, as well, unfortunately so in this case. Discovering no toilet paper in the bathrooms, she rushed out and got some. And you wondered what goes on behind the scenes of a club opening.

We were off and running.

Maria and Noel, both Charlotte jazz fixtures, perform a dozen or so times a year. Maria says she loves that the club is just the right size – big enough to have a good house, small enough to have intimacy. Noel says *Middle C* isn't a bar with music, it's a performance venue that serves drinks. He's played a lot of places, some good, some he wishes he never stepped foot in. Not once, he says, has he performed at *Middle C* and driven home muttering, "Well that sucked."

Saxophonist Ziad Rabie, a Bechtler and *Middle C* mainstay, is part of the family. We bring in national acts like saxophonist Ronnie Laws, vocalist Sy Smith (she plays with the great trumpet player Chris Botti), flutist Alexander Zonjic and pianist (and child prodigy) Joey Alexander. At his age, I could barely stumble through "Hava Nagila" on the keyboards. We've tried to give customers a sense of what's coming. For example, two Wednesdays a month are dedicated to classic standards – *Remember Whensdays* we call it. Thursday leans toward R&B (the music of Whitney Houston, Luther Vandross and the like). Rodney Shelton and Eric Brice have helped make those evenings a hit. Friday and Saturday are mainstream jazz. Sunday nights are smooth jazz. One Sunday a month, we offer a gospel brunch. John Dillard on bass and Tim Scott on drums have made Sundays flourish, organizing and performing at the shows. See the schedule for yourself at www.middlecjazz.com.

Maria Howell, Noel Freidline, Middle C.

We've struck a chord with our clientele by offering tribute and theme shows under the umbrella of jazz. Maria headlines a *Girls In Gowns* show once a year, taking the stage with several women to perform a variety of music from the American songbook to gospel. Noel performs a Dave Brubeck tribute show. For Valentine's Day, Maria and Noel team up on love songs. We've honored the legendary Ray Charles and Stevie Wonder. How memorable was this? Robyn Charles, the youngest of Ray Charles' children, shared with us a video introduction to the *Catching Some Rays* tribute to her dad, thanking us for honoring her father. In the future, I want to hold a talent show for young musicians and/or a jam session to give the artists of tomorrow a stage today.

We've caught on with artists. Maria says she frequently hears from performers wanting to know, "Can I get a gig at *Middle C*?" To have a club like this in her hometown (actually next to her hometown of Gastonia), Maria tells me she's thankful to have a seat at the party.

Members of the *Middle C* family all have their favorite moments.

Teddy Johnson, our managing director, remembers the woman who approached him at the end of one of our shows after COVID-19 restrictions were relaxed. She was singing and laughing and thanked him for giving her something to look forward to amid a year of fear and loneliness.

Noel Freidline remembers the shows that he and his quartet performed with Maria and actor Keith David. There was a blend of music (including Nat King Cole classics) and spoken word so powerful that the evenings took on a life of its own.

I hope you'll come to *Middle C* and enjoy a night of jazz as much as I do. Several nights a week, I'll drop by. I'll kibbitz with the customers, many of whom are friends and regulars. I love looking out onto the audience and seeing patrons of all ages, cultures, color and hometowns. Credit for such diversity belongs to jazz. I'll greet the band, check in with the staff and see if there are any fires to put out. In the club business, there are always fires to put out. Then I'll take a seat and take it all in, Ella and Frank, Count Basie and the Duke reborn, a legacy come to life.

"Holy ----," I'll say to myself. "This is what I wanted."

A final personal reflection: *Middle C* goes deeper than intending the club to be my gift to the city where I was born and raised. It's my opportunity to share a dream and many nights of jazz with two of our sons, Adam and Reid. Harrison, our middle son, would be part of this except he's in Phoenix, Arizona, working on his medical residency in neurosurgery, married to Julia Gray, raising their infant son, Sam.

Adam and Reid have their own lives, their own careers. But for them to be part of *Middle C* – planning, executing and enjoying it with their father – you parents out there can understand what that means to me. It's a blessing.

There's a reason why each chapter of my story ends with a list of people who have helped me make music. More than any other business, music is a collaborative effort. It takes a team of people with passion, creativity and courage to deliver the sounds that fill our lives.

At *Middle C*, the investors who believed in the project included Adam Farber, Andrew Conroy, Andrew Quartapella, Barry Ezarsky, David Crane, David Kossove, Dennis Smith, Ed Duncan, Frank Scibelli, Jay Chambers, Jonathan Howard, Jonathan Swope, Tom Hager, Tyler Hager, Kara Hager Dunstan, Scott Dunstan, Keith Stoneman, Peter Keane, Randy Stone, Joanne Stone, Wink Rea, Delano Little, Marc Rash, Steve Davis, Wellford Tabor and Yih-Han Ma.

Vendors who helped bring the club to life: Paul Liles (Liles Construction), The Public House (Chris Healy, Delano Little and staff), Colliers International, Robbie Branstrom Adams, d3 Studio architecture, Jonathan Gellman, Missy Hoopingarner (controller), Lynn O'Rourke (controller), Brian Heffron (Comedy Zone owner and a great adviser to me), Charles and Fred Whitfield, Jessica Graham (Fionix Consulting), Ronald Melamed and Wade Sample (Moore & Van Allen), our current attorney Mickey Aberman, Paragon Sound, Plate Perfect Catering, Katie Howson, Josh Torn (Nice Grizzly), SeedSpark and Katie Levans.

The wonderful people present and past who have helped welcome you to the club, serve you food and drinks and make sure the experience was and is awesome: Teddy Johnson, Lizzie Taylor, Cree White, Sean Urquhart, John Brighton, Scott Homewood, Dani Stavropoulos, Reid Farber, Katie Rothweiler, Mel Gray and Shayla Abbott. A heartfelt thank you to each and every one of you.

Bass player John Dillard, Middle C.

Aretha Franklin, 2012.

CHAPTER 5
A LIFETIME OF STORIES

A lifetime ago, I saw the baby grand piano in my friend Craig Madans' house and knew where I was headed. In the blink of an eye, I'm trying to convince Aretha Franklin to take the stage with a broken heart. Arranging for Sheryl Crow to meet a cheerleading friend from back home in Missouri. Putting on a fake long beard to inform patrons that ZZ Top had to cancel that evening's show.

Sometimes I pinch myself and say, "How did all this happen to a kid from Charlotte, North Carolina?"

Booking acts, promoting shows, even opening a jazz club, you can plan for that kind of thing. But in the music business, it's the stuff that comes out of nowhere – wacky and unique – that makes a life in my world rewarding. As I recalled one story after another for this chapter, I found myself saying "I love this one!" I hope you love them, too – vignettes that offer insights into what these stars are really like. In a few places I left out names to protect the innocent and, come to think of it, the guilty. That includes the musical legend who flirted with women from the stage, then backstage, all in front of their men.

At 10 p.m. the night before Aretha Franklin was to perform at *Music With Friends* on February 11, 2012, I got a call from her people. Aretha, whose voice is a gift from God, wasn't going on. The singer (and friend) she had known since childhood, Whitney Houston, had just died unexpectedly. Aretha, her representative told me, was in no condition to perform. I felt her pain. But I also felt an obligation to the audience eager to see and hear the Queen of Soul. Aretha grew up singing in church. McGlohon Theater, where she would perform, is an old Baptist church rich in warmth and intimacy. Where better to perform than here, I told Aretha's team. Why not take the stage and honor Whitney in song? That's what happened. Forty-five minutes into her set, seated at the piano, orchestra and backup singers behind her, Aretha offered a gospel-tinged tribute to Whitney. I'll never forget it. Neither will those in the audience. Performing a plaintive, improvisational version of Whitney's classic "I Will Always Love You," she half sung and half reminisced. "We want to say thank you"..."Jesus loves me"..."Pray for the family"..."She was a daughter, a wife, a Christian, a singer"...These spontaneous moments live on the Internet. Thank you, Aretha. A side note to the night: Before Aretha went on, I paid part of her fee in cash – $50,000 in 50 wrappers, each holding $1,000. There's a poignant legacy to this, going back to when some promoters would cheat artists out of what they were due. As we sat together backstage counting the money, Aretha and I shared 10 wonderful minutes of conversation. She talked about Whitney's passing and the recent Grammy Awards. When we were done, Aretha stuffed the $50,000 in

CHAPTER 5

Aretha, 2012.

James Taylor, Democratic National Convention, Charlotte, 2012.

cash in her pocketbook, walked on stage and set it on the piano, never letting it out of her sight. Then she performed.

While we're on the subject, I booked James Brown for a concert in Roanoke, Va., in 1993 put on by First Union. The Godfather of Soul himself. I knocked on his door before the show to give him his $25,000 check. You guessed it. He wanted cash only. He didn't care if it was Sunday. And if the cash didn't arrive in time? That old adage isn't true. The show must not go on. So a bunch of us toting grocery bags hit every ATM machine we could find and came up with $25,000. "Mr.

Brown," I said, "here's your cash." Because he had to be on stage in five minutes, he didn't have time to count it. Trust me, it was all there. He played the gig. It was great. He was The Godfather of Soul after all.

People are always asking me "What is so-and-so *really* like?" It's as if some of us hunger to learn that this star is spoiled or that star is obnoxious. A lifetime of experience has taught me that most artists are regular people who want what you and I want in life. Kindness. Respect. Privacy. They want to talk about where they're from, and their kids and families, the things we all love talking about. When it comes time for a *Meet And Greet* with the crowd, usually before the show, they patiently pose for photos, shake hands, sign an old record album and accommodate the fans if it's reasonable. Tony Bennett, Chicago and ZZ Top were all great at *Meet And Greets*. It's a lot like life: Every so often you'll encounter a diva or jerk. The managers who represent the stars can get prickly. But the stars and legends? Practice the Golden Rule – *Treat others as you want to be treated* – and you'll get the best from them.

Now back to the stories.

I've always done my best to give out-of-town performers the hospitality they deserve, whether it's great food and accommodations or a first-class dressing room. I want them to feel that they've never been treated better than we treated them in Charlotte. Typically, my job is to pick them up at the airport and take them to the hotel, pointing out our city's landmarks as we go. James Taylor, one of my all-time heroes, had other plans. In town in 2008 to perform for wealth management clients during the Wachovia golf tournament at Quail Hollow Club, he needed something when he landed. A harmonica. So I drove him to the Sam Ash Music Store on Tyvola Road and sat in the car while he went inside and bought a harmonica. I wonder if the clerk at the register knew who he or she was ringing up? Driving James was like riding with a buddy – no pretenses. We talked about our Chapel Hill connections. I attended school there, he grew up there. His dad, Dr. Isaac Taylor, was dean of the med school. James told me that when he decided to head to New York in search of a life in music, his mom Gertrude, cheered him on. His dad, as many dads will do, was supportive but worried whether his son would make it. He need not have worried. His son and all his siblings (including Livingston and Kate) fared just fine in music. On that same visit to Charlotte, James and his band did the usual sound check at the venue, Amos' Southend on South Tryon Street, which turned into a three-hour rehearsal. I sat there listening to them run through "Carolina in My Mind" and all the rest and thought to myself, "Larry Farber, what did you do in life to deserve this?"

When I think of James Taylor I think of his friend, Carole King. Google them performing "You've Got a Friend." It's amazing. Carole was out of our price range for *Music With Friends*, but she did come to town in 2014 to do a small benefit for 50 people in support of Sen. Kay Hagan and other Democratic women running for U.S Senate. My friend, Rabbi Judy Schindler, and I were standing in the hosts' home, 10 feet from Carole as she performed "You've Got a Friend" with a twist. That evening, she sang "You've Got a Friend in Kay Hagan." Judy says it was as if Carole was singing just for us, sharing the songs we sung out loud growing up. Judy to this day calls it a surreal experi-

Crosby, Stills & Nash with Adam, Sarah, Julia Gray, Harrison and Larry, 2010.

ence. Another memory: I remember Carole telling us she was terrified to see "Beautiful," the musical playing on Broadway at the time celebrating her life and music. But she mustered the courage to see the show one evening. There was no fanfare to her visit. At the curtain call, she walked on stage and joined the stunned cast in singing.........You know what they sang. A postscript: We lost Kay Hagan to illness in 2019.

Who said artists are needy?

I already shared in Chapter 3 how Michael McDonald needed a dentist before his *Music With Friends* show. Before their 2010 *Music With Friends* show, Stephen Stills of Crosby, Stills & Nash needed a chiropractor. (No jokes about how old they are, please, I love these guys). We found one. Stephen had a one-hour massage. He was good to go. Another artist who shall remain nameless requested painkillers before he went on. We got him a placebo instead. He took it. It must have done whatever he wanted done. He performed and did just fine. I don't know, or want to know, anything more.

Some artists have specific requests, or should I say demands. We booked Dionne Warwick to appear as the mystery celebrity guest at the opening of Levine Children's Hospital in 2007. She was going to perform a 60-minute show, plenty of time to do her hits like "Do You Know the Way to San Jose." "Time" was the operative word. Her manager informed us that she was going on at the exact moment her contract called for no matter what else was happening on stage. Dionne took the stage as they were thanking benefactors. Somehow it worked because people though it was planned, as in "Here comes the mystery celebrity guest." Dionne honored another clause in her contract. No encores no matter how loudly the audience clapped for one.

There are requests and then there are requests.

For her 2011 *Music With Friends* show, Diana Ross asked for a movie or video to watch during the two hours she took to do her own makeup and wardrobe. We arranged for her to watch a tape of an Earth, Wind & Fire concert. We also had to build a change booth because her show had five costume changes. Here again, Diana Ross has what I believe to be an unfair reputation for being a diva. I found her gracious. Her only request? She preferred being called Miss Ross.

When he got to town for his 2009 Loggins & Messina show, Kenny Loggins needed a guitar. Don't ask me what happened to his. We got one from Rick McClanahan, who plays with Coconut Groove, a band

Diana Ross, 2011.

Kenny Loggins, 2009.

that's under the EastCoast Entertainment banner. Kenny liked the guitar so much he bought it the next day.

Christopher Cross, who performed on a *Music With Friends* bill with America in 2016, once wrote a song about a past love. That past love now lived in Charlotte. He asked us to find her and invite her to the show so they could reconnect at the concert venue. Mission accomplished.

Sheryl Crow, here for *Music With Friends* in 2010, wanted to reunite with a cheerleading friend from Missouri who had settled in Charlotte. We made it happen. It's part of giving artists the experience of a

Darius Rucker, 2012.

lifetime. Funny story that could have been not so funny if the star was less classy: Up drives Sheryl Crow's tour bus and out steps the star. Only she's not wearing makeup or stage clothes. She sees me and says, "I'm here for the show." I respond, "And you are?..." She laughed about it. I'm not sure I did at the time.

Here's an artist's request I'll never forget fulfilling. I go back with Darius Rucker to his Hootie & the Blowfish days. In 2011, when he found out Bonnie Raitt was playing *Music With Friends*, he asked me to ask her if they could sing "Angel From Montgomery" together.

Bonnie and John Prine made that duet a classic. "Hell yeah," Bonnie said. Darius played a show in Las Vegas, chartered a private jet, flew all night to Charlotte and performed the song unrehearsed with Bonnie as a surprise encore. The crowd loved it. Bonnie's another favorite of mine, down to earth, as you can imagine based on her earthy music and vibe. When she found out that "I Can't Make You Love Me" is one of my all-time favorites, she caught my eye and smiled as she performed it at *Music With Friends* in Houston.

Another one I won't forget: When Joe Walsh needed a private plane to fly from Teterboro, N.J., to Charlotte for his *Music With Friends* show in 2015, Rick Hendrick came to the rescue. The businessman, NASCAR team owner and *Music With Friends* member arranged to chauffeur Walsh on one of his private jets. Rick even furnished a car for me to get Joe to the show. Rick's "fee?" A guitar autograph by Walsh. Done.

You never know where the requests will come from.

When Sheik Mohammed Hussein Al Amoudi needed a headliner for the 1998 opening of the luxury Sheraton Addis in Addis Ababa, Ethiopia, I got them Kool & the Gang. I couldn't make it to the show as much as I wanted to. I later found out that the funk and soul legends went on at 2 a.m. I don't think the band's fee was a problem. The hotel cost $200 million to build.

Audience members sometimes make requests. In 2012, Daryl Hall of Hall & Oates ("Rich Girl," "Sara Smile" and more) asked if he could perform a duet with Smokey Robinson when the Motown legend played Charleston. Seems like they did "My Girl." Fast forward to Charleston in 2015. One patron celebrating his 65th birthday at the

Hall & Oates show asked to go backstage to meet them. We made that patron's night. Bill Murray. In Nashville in 2013, I took Connie Britton (from TV's "Nashville," "Dirty John," "Friday Night Lights" and more) backstage to meet Diana Ross. In Nashville in 2015, I took Amy Grant (a great Christian singer and Vince Gill's wife) backstage to meet Kenny Loggins.

You put on shows for a living, you're going to have problems.

When Jackson Browne came to town in 2008 with an Obama sticker plastered on his piano, a handful of *Music With Friends* patrons canceled their membership. Can't music rise above partisanship if only long enough for us enjoy "Doctor My Eyes" together?

When Huey Lewis & the News canceled their 2018 date two days before the show, we managed to line up the rock band Styx to take the stage. A postscript: Huey Lewis had to bow out due to Meniere's Disease, the inner ear malady that has threatened his career. We're thinking good thoughts for him.

When ZZ Top canceled one day before their 2018 show – one of the founding members took ill – there was no time to find a replacement. *Music With Friends* colleague and friend Becky Mitchener joined me in calling all 550 patrons to break the news. That's not all. Becky and I put on fake, long ZZ Top-like beards and waited at McGlohon Theater in case anyone hadn't heard. We probably could have taken a whack at "Sharp Dressed Man," but fortunately for anyone who might have had to listen to us, no one showed up. The beards are history, thank goodness. A sad footnote: Dusty Hill, the bassist for ZZ Top, passed away as I worked on this book. His passing reminds me to

Katie Couric, her daughter's wedding, 2021.

embrace every encounter with an artist, for life is fleeting.

The seeds of this book were planted as the result of the birth of our three grandchildren, Sutton, Mac and Sam. As I counted my blessings, I thought about all the stories that are part of who I am. I can't bear to lose them to time. I have written them down here so that long after my voice is stilled, memories of the music will live on.

I saved my best wedding booking for last. Fourth of July 2021, a sunny day on a mountaintop at Cedar Lake Estate in Port Jervis, N.Y. The groom was a lovely young man, Mark Dobrosky. The bride was a beautiful young woman and talented TV screenwriter, Ellie Monahan. *You may know her as Katie Couric's daughter.* What a thrill for me. I've spent years booking wedding bands for EastCoast Entertainment. One of our most popular bands is Big Swing and the Ballroom Blasters. Katie heard them previously at the wedding of her college roommate's daughter and wanted them for Ellie's wedding. That's how I got to work with Katie for two years – COVID canceled the original wedding date in 2020. Over numerous texts and Zoom calls, we talked about the music. She is among the most gracious celebrities with whom I've worked. To top it all off, she insisted I attend. That's how I got to spend Fourth of July among 250 guests at a wedding that was both lavish and warm. I'm precluded from sharing the names of celebrities who attended. But I can tell you that when I introduced myself to Katie (we had never met in person), she gave me a hug and kiss and asked me to tie a bow on her wrist. Under an arbor, the bride and groom exchanged vows they each had written. Katie's wedding toast moved everyone to tears, reminiscing about her late husband Jay, who was Ellie's dad. Dinner was in a converted barn, roast chicken and halibut served family style. The band was great. The couple danced their first dance to Frankie Valli's "Can't Take My Eyes Off You." Ellie told People magazine that her husband did his first good deed during the dance. Someone had dropped their margarita on the dance floor and Mark avoided the broken glass as he led Ellie around. The party included Fourth of July fireworks over the lake. My unforgettable experience ended a few days later with a thank you email from Ellie and a text from Katie saying she was going to sleep for a week. A personal postscript: This is probably the last wedding band I'll book. It was the first in which my flight to the wedding was canceled at the last minute and I wound up driving 10 hours to the venue. Made it with 20 minutes to spare. And the band? Its bus broke down on the way home to Atlanta. They wound up camping out in a Hampton Inn lobby waiting for it to be fixed.

I remember the day in 2007 when Tony Bennett walked into Spirit Square and spotted the portrait of Loonis McGlohon hanging above the arch. McGlohon Theater at Spirit Square is named for the jazz great from Charlotte. Tony immediately recognized the portrait. Turns out he had worked with Loonis decades ago on an NPR radio series. Turns out, too, that Tony is an artist. His eyes settled on the hands in the portrait and the care with which the artist painted them. Two legends, one moment. When Tony played *Music With Friends* in Houston, his daughter, singer Antonia Bennett, opened the show. When it came Tony's turn, I noticed Antonia sitting backstage, listening. I'll never forget what she said: "As long as he's out there singing, I will be right there savoring each moment." Me, too.

I played golf one summer day in 2012 with Darius Rucker, Philip Bailey of Earth, Wind & Fire and my friend, Cantey Hare, at Bulls Bay Golf Club outside Charleston. Darius is serious about the game. He was on the driving range when we arrived. Philip was just learning the game. That didn't stop Darius from trying to make a few side bets. More than the golf, I appreciate our time together. Here I was with Darius, who made it big in rock and then in country music (not easy for an African American). And here I was with one of his idols, Philip, whose R&B/funk/soul band blazed a trail for performers like Darius. I have been blessed to develop a personal friendship with Philip. We've shared golf, meals and afternoons on a boat. I was honored to join in a Zoom birthday celebration for him. He is everything you'd want in a friend – quiet, humble, respectful. A diva he is not.

I remember the exuberance and grace of so many artists.

When Steely Dan came to play *Music With Friends* in 2009, the jazz rock band's co-founder, Walter Becker, took sound check to new heights. He came down from the stage and positioned himself in a dozen or more spots around the theater. He wanted to make sure the sound was pristine for everyone. Cancer took him in 2017 at age 67. Every time I hear "Reelin' in the Years," I can see Walter roaming the theater in search of perfection.

When Gladys Knight came to town in 2007, she brought a guest performer: The Bowie State University Marching Band, high-stepping down the aisle. When I think of Gladys, I think of "Midnight Train to Georgia" and that marching band.

When jazz singer Al Jarreau performed on a bill with George Benson in 2008. I remember how he prepared for the show. He gathered his band in a circle, they held hands and prayed. Al was 76 when he passed away in 2017.

When Darius Rucker played *Music With Friends* in 2012, we learned that a couple in the audience had lost their daughter in a car accident. She was on the way to baby-sit. It turns out her favorite singer was Darius. We arranged for the bereaved couple and artist to spend several moments talking backstage, a reminder that music can touch our souls.

Touch our souls.

In 2012, I got the chance to spend time with Glenn Frey, a founding member of the Eagles. We booked him to play Charlotte one night, Charleston the next. Over dinner one night at BLT Steak in The Ritz-Carlton uptown, he spoke of how special it was to play intimate venues like ours compared to arenas and stadiums. We were joined that evening by another musical giant. Bill Szymczyk, one of America's great record producers, worked on The Eagles' iconic "Hotel California." That album won the Grammy for Record of the Year in 1978. As we went over details for the upcoming shows, Glenn said to me, "Whatever you want me to do, Boss." Glenn Frey – an Eagle, the guy who cowrote one of the great rock songs of all time, "Desperado" – called me Boss. Those are the nights I think about that kid from Charlotte, North Carolina, spotting the baby grand piano in my friend's home and deciding to follow the music.

I had a minute with Glenn Frey.

Four years later, he died at age 67.

That minute lives on. So does the music. So do the stories.

Glenn Frey, 2012.

Jay Thomas, New York, 2016.

CHAPTER 6

MY FRIEND JAY

Let me take you back to one night around midnight in 1974. It's closing time at The Boardwalk, the beach music club I own on Monroe Road. The lights go up and I see a guy crawling around on his hands and knees. Immediately I recognize him as the morning deejay on Big WAYS Radio here in Charlotte. At the time, he was making a name for himself with his crazy shtick. I tap him on the shoulder and say, "Can I help you?" He tells me he's looking for a $50 bill he dropped sometime that evening. He can't find it. "Let me look in the cash register," he says, "I'll recognize it." Nice try. I pass. "If you need it that bad," I say, "I'll buy you breakfast." At 1:30 in the morning, we share a meal at the old Knife & Fork on Independence. I pick up the tab (of course). He invites me back to his apartment at The Chimneys to continue the conversation. I walk in to find a living room full of blow-up furniture. He grabs a bicycle pump, fills a chair with air and says "Sit down."

It was Jay Thomas. That was the beginning of our beautiful friendship.

You know Jay as the comedian and actor who co-starred on such TV classics as "Cheers" and "Murphy Brown." I know him as my best friend. He loved my family like his own. I loved his family the same way. We shared our ups and downs, personally and professionally. We played a ton of tennis. Whether it was at Charlotte's Cedar Forest Racquet Club in the old days or at Jay's homes in Greenwich, Connecticut, or Santa Barbara, California, after he made it big, he could never beat me. I sat in the audience and watched him make America laugh during his annual Christmas appearance on "Late Show with David Letterman." To this day, I cannot hear the words "The Lone Ranger" without cracking up. I'll explain in a bit. I must have been living right the day I chose to watch him film his first big TV show, "Mork & Mindy," starring an up-and-coming comic actor named Robin Williams. Raquel Welch was the guest star.

My best friend – Jay, not Raquel – was the funniest guy in the room no matter who else was in the room. His battery never wore down. He could make you laugh until you cried. Because he had no filter, sometimes he'd make you cringe until you cried. He was not quiet (by any means) but he was reflective. He was loyal to his friends, and to Charlotte because this is where he began to shine. Amid our travels and adventures – watching the ACC Tournament on TV in Las Vegas or my sons' football games at Charlotte Country Day School – we'd share our hopes, plans, faults and schemes. We'd toss a football whether it was at halftime of the County Day games or someplace else, for that was Jay's trademark and love. And we'd laugh. A lot.

Let me tell you about Jay. I think of him every day, and each time

Jay and Larry, 1984.

I pick up the phone. I can't bear to erase the voicemail his wife, Sally, left me on August 24, 2017, telling me that cancer had taken him. He was 69.

Growing up in New Orleans, Jay got hooked early by performing. He was doing standup on Bourbon Street when he was 16. Taken by Jay's natural motormouth, Charlotte's Stan Kaplan hired him for WAPE, a radio station he owned in Jacksonville, Fla. He moved Jay to Charlotte in the early 1970s to be the morning deejay on Big WAYS Radio. Unless you were living here at the time, you can't appreciate how big Jay and the station became, and how fast. He was one of the first of the over-the-top morning radio personalities, doing impersonations and screwball routines, playing off his sidekick, the considerably saner Larry Sprinkle. Jay and Larry remained close until the end. Shortly before Jay died, Larry and I joined him at the TPC Piper Glen golf club to share some laughs. You don't often see friendships that profound in show business. I gave us nicknames. I was L1 and Larry Sprinkle was L2. Way back when, Jay tried to lure L2 to bigger markets. Charlotte's good fortune. L2 (Larry Sprinkle), our favorite weatherman and a huge supporter of local charities, stayed put. Jay left for a radio job in New York and eventually another radio gig in Los Angeles. He had his own Sirius XM show until he fell ill. Jay used to fill in for shock jock Howard Stern on Howard's Sirius radio show on Fridays. A month before Jay died, Howard called Jay and told him how he used to pull off the side of the road to listen and learn from Jay's bits. Jay was a radio legend.

By the time Jay left Charlotte for bigger things – our city couldn't contain his gifts – our friendship was growing. He'd return often for visits, usually staying at our home or the home of his longtime accountant, Hal Curry. If I called and asked Jay to appear at this benefit for my synagogue, Temple Beth El, or that event, he'd oblige. One time I asked him to introduce Crosby, Stills & Nash at a *Music With Friends* show. He made a way-too-personal joke about one of the artists. The artist got ticked off. That was Jay. No filter. I never let anyone introduce a *Music With Friends* act again. Most of all, our connection was sustained by how proud we were of each other, and by knowing we were each other's best friends. Life, I learned, is built on relationships and brightened by stories (and music). Jay blessed my life with both.

I've stifled tears working on this chapter. But I did it because sharing Jay's journey is worth it.

The break that catapulted Jay from deejay to TV sitcom mainstay came in 1979 when he joined the cast of "Mork & Mindy" for two seasons. His goofiness, pesky smile, not to mention that white man's Afro – radio couldn't do it justice. Jay had this look, like he was always cooking up something so you better keep an eye on him. You could see Jay's success coming fast. He played Remo DaVinci, whose New York deli became a hangout for Mork and Monday. Jay beat out a comic named Jay Leno for the part. The Friday I watched them film (yes, the episode with Raquel Welch), Robin Williams warmed up the studio audience. You could see the genius beginning to come out in him. Robin might have been the only person who ever intimidated Jay, such was his gift. Jay also became good friends with Pam Dawber, who played Mindy. After filming, the cast would hit the L.A. comedy clubs. It's difficult recalling this part of Jay's story knowing how the story ended, with Robin's eventual death by suicide.

Remember Jay's turn on "Cheers?" It started in the show's fifth season in 1987. He played hockey goalie Eddie LeBec, who eventually marries wiseacre waitress Carla Tortelli, played by Rhea Perlman. Jay

Jay and Mork (Robin Williams).

loved being on that show, loved Rhea, Woody Harrelson and everyone else in the cast. You could tell by watching the show how close the cast had become. It was like watching real-life bar patrons, not actors. Jay would toss a football between scenes with the star of the show, Ted Danson. How the role ended is pure Jay. During a radio interview, Jay told a joke in jest that he shouldn't have, about having to kiss Rhea on the show. Again, no filter. Rhea was listening. They wrote Jay out of the show. He was run over by a Zamboni at an ice show.

Another prominent role came in 1989 when he played Jerry Gold, a sleazy talk show host and Candice Bergen's romantic interest in the comedy "Murphy Brown." Google the episode in which Jay is dressed in a shark costume and Murphy says to him, "Is that a harpoon in your pocket or are you just glad to see me?" Jay's smile, equal parts joyful and sly, said it all. Jay won two Emmys on that show and got to work with a legend in Bergen. He thought she was all class. I'll never forget the day he called to tell me he was doing a kissing scene with her. "Larry," he said, "I looked in her eyes and said to myself, 'I've never kissed anyone else like this.' Unfortunately, she was thinking the same thing."

Jay did a lot more in his career. He starred in a well-reviewed sit-com in the early 1990s, "Love & War," playing newspaper columnist Jack Stein opposite Susan Dey and then Annie Potts. He played Bill Meister, the school's football coach, in "Mr. Holland's Opus." Starring Richard Dreyfuss, the 1995 film tells the story of a small-town music teacher who finally realizes he's been living his dream. It's a tearjerker but a lovely one. Dreyfuss appreciated the gift of improvisation that Jay brought to the film. In 2003, Jay performed in an Off-Broadway comedy, "Writer's Block," directed by Woody Allen. I'm not making this up (re: the web of sexual allegations that have swirled around Woody for years). The play was about marital infidelity. Jay told me that the entire time Woody was directing him, he never looked directly at Jay. Woody's head was always down. No one ever said Woody was average. There were other credits, including guest spots on various TV shows,

Jay and Dave Letterman, the famous football-tossing bit.

among them "Law & Order: Special Victims Unit" and (ugh) "Love Boat." Jay rightfully earned a star on the Hollywood Walk of Fame. None of this, at least to me, is as powerful a part of Jay's legacy as his annual Christmas appearances on Letterman. It was hilarious when they were happening. With Jay gone, those appearances are hilarious and tender.

Christmas 1998. Dave invited New York Jets quarterback Vinny Testaverde (he later played for our Panthers) to throw a football and knock a meatball from the top of the tree where the star is supposed to go. Vinny missed. That's when Jay, a former small college quarterback, appeared from the celebrities' green room, grabbed the football and

The Farbers and Thomases, New York, 2008.

down came the meatball. The crowd, and Dave, went crazy. A Christmas tradition was born. Every year from 1998 to 2014 (except 2013), Jay did the football-knocks-the-meatball-from-the-tree routine.

That wasn't all. Each Christmas appearance, Jay also told what Dave called The Greatest Talk Show Story Of All Time. It hurts me to have it paraphrase, but here goes: Back when he was a deejay at Big WAYS, Jay would do remotes at car dealerships, as many disc jockeys do. At one promotion in Charlotte, the station hired Clayton Moore to make a guest appearance in full costume. Moore was best known as The Lone Ranger, the iconic TV show cowboy/hero from yesteryear. It's still on in reruns more than 60 years after it first aired. Jay and The

Lone Ranger did their bit at the dealership, then Jay and a friend, Mike Martin, stepped behind a dumpster to get "herbed up, medically enhanced" as he told Letterman every year. When The Lone Ranger's ride back to the Red Carpet Inn on East Morehead Street didn't show up, Jay and Mike wound up chauffeuring The Lone Ranger in Jay's 10-year-old beat-up Volvo filled with crap. Stuck in traffic, another driver hit Jay's Volvo and broke his headlight. Jay chased the knuckle-head down. The two drivers got out of their cars. "You ran into me and broke my headlight," Jay screamed. The other driver responded, "No, I didn't." Jay threatened to call the cops. The man called Jay's bluff. "Who are the police going to believe, me or you two stoned hippies?" That's when The Lone Ranger stepped out of the car, six guns, silver bullets and all, and declared, "They'll believe me, citizen."

It's classic Jay, funny and quirky in an innocent way. I crack up every time. Two poignant postscripts. Number one. When Jay was too sick to tell the story on Letterman in 2016, Dave invited tennis legend John McEnroe to do the honors. Word for word, John did it like Jay did it. Jay called McEnroe to thank him. Number two. A week or so before Jay died, I pulled some strings and arranged to have Dave call Jay. They reminisced about The Lone Ranger story. Then Dave said to Jay "Let's stay in touch." Jay told Dave he didn't think he'd be able to.

I have so many Jay Thomas memories.

When he was at Big WAYS, Jay lived at Providence Square Apartments. Driving to work one morning on Providence Road, I noticed a moving truck outside Jay's apartment, loading up his furniture. This was after his blow-up furniture phase. I called Jay at the studio to tell him. He didn't have a clue. But he quickly got to the bottom of it. His first wife was leaving him. All she left behind was a white suit belonging to Jay and a promotional picture jokingly advertising "Jay for Mayor." The next day, Jay moved into our apartment with my three roommates and me. He slept on the couch. We didn't charge him rent. He paid us back by cooking. Jay could go into the refrigerator, pull out some food and whip up a masterpiece.

Jay's personal life wasn't exactly the stuff of a Hallmark movie. He and his second wife, Sally, were married for 30 years. They had two sons, Jake and Sam. Before they married in 1987, Jay had had a third son, J.T., with another woman. J.T. was given up for adoption. Years later, father and son reunited, then reconciled. A highlight of my life came in December 2008. I took two of my sons – Adam, then 21, and Harrison, then 18 – to New York to watch Jay film the Letterman show. Jay brought two of his sons – Sam and J.T. – to join us. I'll never forget walking onto the stage of the Ed Sullivan Theater where Letterman filmed his show. Here is where Sullivan filmed his legendary variety show decades ago. I'm a music guy, a child of the 1960s. "I was overcome with emotion. "The friggin' Beatles were here!" I said to the boys. It was Feb. 9, 1964, and their first American TV appearance catapulted The Beatles to stardom and beyond. The boys, being mere boys, didn't grasp the significance of the moment to their old man. Later, the boys and I sat in the audience and watched Jay tell The Lone Ranger story. It never got old. Still doesn't.

Jay filled his four years in Charlotte with lots of funny stuff. Trying to seize on his celebrity, the Kaplans had Jay do color commentary

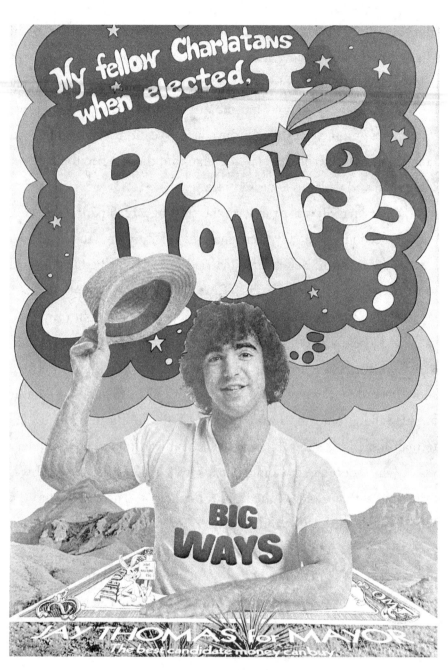

Jay "running" for Charlotte mayor, Big WAYS shtick.

on radio broadcasts of the UNC Charlotte basketball games. Only he didn't know squat about basketball, and the play-by-play guy was John Kilgo, a sports broadcasting legend in these parts known for being lovably irascible. During one broadcast, Jay noted that it looked like the team had switched to a zone defense. Bad guess. As the story goes (true or not, I can't say), Kilgo responded, "You idiot, they're shooting free throws."

Jay and I took some great trips, played a lot of golf and had a blast wherever we went and whatever we did. Once, he and I took his mother, Cathy, and his aunt to Las Vegas to see her idol, Frank Sinatra. Determined to get to the front row, I tipped the maître d' enough to make it happen. When Jay was involved, you never knew who might show up. We used to go to Super Bowls. In 1993, we flew to Pasadena, California, and watched the Dallas Cowboys clobber Buffalo. Our group included myself, Jay, Jay's friend Frank Pace, former NBA star Artis Gilmore and Stedman Graham. Yes, Oprah's long-term boyfriend. On a few of our annual forays to Vegas to watch the ACC tournament on TV (really an excuse to play golf and have fun), our group included some of my frat brothers from UNC Chapel Hill and Jay's physician, Dr. Rob Huizenga. Google him. He testified for the defense at the O.J. Simpson trial, having examined Simpson three days after the murders at the behest of the defense. He was also the doctor for the NFL's Oakland Raiders (now in L.A.) and wrote a novel about the NFL, "Any Given Sunday," that was turned into a movie of the same name. He also appeared on "The Biggest Loser" reality TV show. Most importantly for us, he was fun to hang out with in Vegas. Even though

I subscribe to the edict "What happens in Vegas, stays in Vegas," I'll share this Jay Thomas moment. One night, eight of us went for dinner to the famed Bacchanal Room at Caesars Palace, where hostesses dressed as Cleopatra and the male staff as Roman soldiers. That was the only cue Jay needed to put some getup up on his head and stand on the chair. He was playing the part of a Roman soldier. If I had done it, we've have been thrown out. Or the chair would have collapsed. But it was classic Jay. Everyone in the crowded restaurant laughed.

One more Jay-in-a-restaurant story. Jay, my wife Sherri and I were having dinner one night at Blue in uptown Charlotte. The night we were there, Jay spilled a drop of red wine on a beautifully starched white dress shirt. He proceeded to intentionally spill every other sauce and condiment he could find on the shirt. He could have fingerpainted on his shirt. Everyone laughed and stared, which is what Jay was after, that night and always. Sherri wound up spending several hours removing the stains. I don't recall her laughing.

One more story, this one also involving Sherri. We were in California visiting Jay at his Hollywood Hills home. He was taking us on a tour of the house. There was no blow-up furniture. Even though it was late and his wife, Sally, was eight months pregnant and asleep, he insisted on showing us the bedroom. "She sleeps like a rock," he said. Not so much. Awakened by her visitors, she screamed to Jay, "What the ---- are you doing?"

When it involved Jay, there was never a dull moment. Never A Dull Moment. That was his legacy. He'd have approved.

We end where we began, where my friendship with Jay Thomas began, at The Boardwalk on Monroe Road late that night in 1974. Turns out he really did lose $50. And while he never found it and couldn't convince me to hand him one from the cash register, our midnight encounter led to something more profound than money.

A few weeks before Jay died, I flew to California for one last visit. We talked about a thousand things, including that long-lost $50. We said goodbye. I cried all the way from his Santa Barbara home to Los Angeles International Airport. When I got back to Charlotte, I bought a birthday card for Jay. He had just turned 69. In the card, I enclosed a new $50 bill and wrote that I had had it all these years and was returning it now without interest. A few days later, he called to tell me it was the greatest gift he had ever received.

Enid (left) and Robyn Farber, around 1961.

CHAPTER 7
REPAIRING THE WORLD

God has blessed me in many ways. I've always believed I am obligated to share those blessings by practicing *Tikkun Olam*. It's the guiding principle of my Jewish faith. "Repair The World."

I support the lost and hurting with my prayers and financial support. I can't give as much as some others, but I am thankful I can give more than most. But writing a check isn't enough. Why not use the skills I possess – building relationships, brainstorming new ideas, bringing people together – to help repair the world? The cause of helping our neighbors can always use a good promoter.

I don't really care that my name won't be on buildings and highways. If I am remembered at all, I want it to be for helping my neighbor and serving my community. That's all that matters to me.

I credit my parents, Charles and Syd, for raising us in a strong Jewish home, my sisters Enid and Robyn and me. We weren't rich except in the ways that count – family, love, caring for others. That love (and patience) came in handy the summer our family took a

cross-country trip to see the sights and visit relatives (think the Gris-
wolds). The three of us kids were packed like sardines into the back
seat of the Lincoln Town Car we borrowed from my Poppy. What
bonding. What bickering. I remember watching the Jerry Lewis
telethon when I was little and seeing how musicians and comedians
shared their talent to raise money for kids with muscular dystro-
phy. That memory stayed with me, this notion of using your gifts
for good. I grew up in Temple Israel, years later moving to Temple
Beth El to raise our family when Sherri and I were married. I was
Bar Mitzvahed at age 13, served as president of Temple Youth, attended Hebrew School twice a week and had summer fun at Camp
Blue Star in Hendersonville in the N.C. mountains. When I went
to UNC-Chapel Hill, I organized the first Passover Seder at Tau
Epsilon Phi. When I joined a group at a young Jewish leaders con-
ference in Washington, D.C., the skill around which I built my career – making deals – came in handy. We arrived at our hotel and
discovered it was a dump. We had a few hundred dollars, not enough
to check out and check in somewhere else. This was back in the day
when a certain break-in made a certain hotel famous. So I called the
Watergate and convinced the manager to rent us a suite for what we
could afford, around 300 bucks as I recall.

"Pack your friggin' bags," I told the guys. "We're going to the Watergate."

Living out your Jewish faith is important, especially in a city like
Charlotte, where the entire faith community whatever the religion
means so much and does so much. Our tight-knit, fast-growing Jewish

Recognition for helping repair the world.

community has come together to do great things. We built the 54-acre Shalom Park community off Providence Road, the center of Jewish life in the region and a model for other communities. Coming next to the campus is Generations of Shalom Park, an upscale senior community honoring Jewish values. We've given millions to good causes. Our most important institutions and buildings are named for the families that have enriched this city in terms of health care, education, sports, the arts and more – the Blumenthals, Levines, Gorelicks, Skluts, Bernsteins, Silvermans and many others.

I want to do my part.

Over the years, I served on the boards of the Family Center, Fight Night For Kids (raising money for children's charities like Ronald McDonald House) and Men For Change, which benefited the shelter for battered women. I didn't get on these committees to promote my company or network for business. I did it to work and help. I was president of the Carolinas' Thanksgiving Day Parade back when it was a rite of the holidays around here. Recently, leaders with the Trail of History reached out to me. This effort, supported by private funds, involves commissioning bronze statues of Charlotte and Carolinas icons. Among those honored are James B. Duke and William Henry Belk. The statues are placed on Little Sugar Creek Greenway, a prominent place for passersby to learn about our heritage. Rightfully so, a statue is being planned to honor jazz legend Loonis McGlohon, who died in 2002. I loved Loonis and all he meant to music in the Carolinas. When they asked me to help make the statue happen, I couldn't say no. "I couldn't say no" might as well be my middle name.

Above all these causes, it's the Jewish community that has my heart.

Here's how it unfolded. For years, I'd see various Jewish institutions in town – all worthy, all counting on the community's financial support – putting on their own fundraisers. Each one of us in town would be asked to give numerous times. I can't help it, it's the promoter in me. What if, I proposed, the Jewish community came together to put on one big event that would not only raise a lot more money but capture people's imagination in a new and vibrant way? We can still have smaller "fun-raisers" that bring people together. But let's have one great fundraiser to pay for the good works we yearn to do.

As president of Temple Beth El from 2002 to 2004, I set out to make it happen. First thing we needed to do was get everyone on board, because changing a tradition is always hard. I met with Allan Oxman, president of Temple Israel at the time. I met with Lane Ostrow, president of the Jewish Community Center, now known as the

Sandra and Leon Levine Jewish Community Center. There it is again, a family's generosity. The center, located between the two synagogues, is home to Jewish organizations, recreation facilities and more. Our goal was to get all the boards on board, agreeing to surrender their own fundraiser and have this one spectacular event in its place. The goal was to raise $50,000 each for Temple Beth El, Temple Israel and the Jewish Community Center.

Thus was born the *One For All Ball* on Sept. 6, 2003.

Obstacles – as in getting a bunch of different boards to come together for a bold, new venture – I can overcome. That's been the story of my life. Events I can plan. That's another chapter in my life story. We wanted this one to have the wow factor, so we booked The Westin Charlotte uptown, the newest, fanciest hotel at the time. We chose Eric and Lori Sklut as the first recipients of the Blumenthal Lifetime Achievement Award for all they have done for Charlotte. The Levine-Sklut Judaic Library, Jewish Family Services, Loaves & Fishes, Queens University, what haven't they supported in and beyond the Jewish community through their family foundation? The Blumenthal award honors a beautiful man, the late Herman Blumenthal, who with his family has given so much and done so much for Charlotte. The Skluts certainly followed Herman's lead: Eric and Lori agreed to match whatever the event raised. We recruited my friends Jay Thomas and Larry Sprinkle as emcees. Can you think of anyone more fun than those two? We booked Party on the Moon for entertainment – an awesome private party band (part of the EastCoast Entertainment stable) that has played for everyone from President Obama on down.

Larry Sprinkle, Jay and Larry, One For All Ball, Charlotte, 2003.

Dinner, auction items, all of it was over the top. We hired event planner Laurie Sanders to help. We lined up decorators and designers in town to make each table look beautiful and distinctive.

Wow factor? Mission accomplished. The first *One For All Ball*, which had a goal of netting $150,000, drew 600 people and netted $750,000. Rather than the hoped-for $50,000, Temple Beth

El, Temple Israel and the Jewish Community Center each received $250,000. We tried as best as we could to make this event accessible to all while still focused on raising a lot of money. We made sure clergy and staff got free tickets. If you ever go into event planning, here's a tip. The price of admission goes toward covering the cost of the event – rent, food, entertainment and more. Money is made through corporate and individual contributions and sponsorships, auctions and the like. The success of that first and three subsequent *One For All Balls* has been one of the joys of my life. Other *One For All Ball* honorees have included Hal Levinson (2006), the Gorelick family (2008) and past presidents of Temple Beth El, Temple Israel and the Jewish Community Center (2010). In all, these events have raised $2 million for the cause of helping Jewish organizations help repair the world. *Tikkun Olam.* We've created the blueprint for this event. Holding it every other year sounds about right to me. When the time is right, may the ball be reborn.

I wasn't done, far from it.

In 2014, I tweaked the concept and promoted a *One For All Concert* at the Knight Theater uptown starring Jason Alexander. The nebbish we know and love (and laugh at) from *"Seinfeld"* put on a wonderful variety show. Sherri, Jay Thomas and I joined Jason and his agent for dinner uptown at Bernardin's Restaurant at the Ratcliffe. It was worth the bill to see those two guys kibbitz their way through the meal.

How about comedy?

Before the *One For All Ball* came to life, we put on two comedy shows at the Comedy Zone on Independence Boulevard, in 1995 and

1996. They needed catchy names, hence *Laugh 'Til You Plotz* to benefit Temple Beth El. "Plotz" is Yiddish for burst, as in we knew patrons would laugh so hard at Gabe Kaplan and then Jackie Mason the next year that their innards would burst. *Plotz.* I know. Hammy.

Gabe Kaplan headlined the first of our *Laugh 'Til You Plotz* shows. He was a delight. He's best known for starring in the TV sitcom, *"Welcome Back, Kotter,"* which launched the career of some guy named John Travolta. But I think Gabe's first love was and is poker. He's a pro at it, having played in the world's biggest tournaments. We talked mostly about cards during his visit. He also asked us to get a babysitter to watch his kid at the hotel while he performed. We still wonder about that. The kid appeared to be a teenager.

Jackie was – how do I say this? – unique. Raised doing comedy in the Borscht Belt hotels of old, he was daring and profane as in this zinger delivered in that rich Yiddish accent: "Eighty percent of married men cheat in America. The rest cheat in Europe." After his show, which was great, we took him to IHOP near Carolina Place mall. Our party included a female acquaintance of his, decked out in mink despite this being the middle of a Carolinas summer. At one point during the meal, he got up and started interviewing everyone in the place about how they were enjoying their food. What can you say about pancakes? I guess that was Jackie hunting for material. I also remember how his hair dye started running down his face. He looked like a melted candle. Jackie died as I was writing this chapter, on July 24, 2021. He was 93. The New York Times headline declared he "Turned Kvetching Into Comedy Gold." In his glory days, Jackie Mason was a source of pride

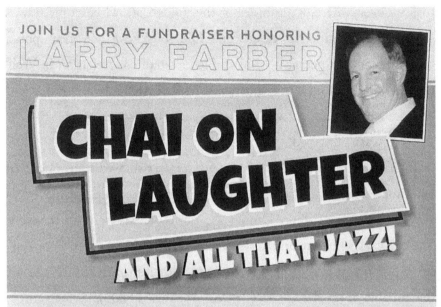

The honor of a lifetime.

to Jews everywhere, a reminder of the golden era when comedy was edgy and witty, not crass or obscene. Did you know that once upon a time he was ordained as a rabbi and led a small congregation in Weldon, N.C., a spot on a map northeast of Raleigh? The rabbinate's loss was the world's gain.

I still wasn't finished.

In 2019, we held the first *Chai On Laughter* show. The Blumenthal Lifetime Achievement Award went to Larry and Dale Polsky, jewels as well. Again, we (Marcy Dumas was our co-chair) went for the wow. The event was held at Spirit Square and featured comedian Paul Reiser. He did a great routine, then sneaked down the street with me for the opening of my *Middle C Jazz Club*. We raised $200,000 for Temple Bethel that evening, far more than the goal of $50,000.

The second *Chai On Laughter & All That Jazz* is set for November 6, 2021, at the newly renovated Sandra Levine Theater at Queens University of Charlotte. It will feature comedian Louie Anderson, funny and poignant as he shares memories of growing up in Minnesota, one of 11 children. Maria Howell, Noel Freidline and friends will perform jazz. I love having them as part of the event, and part of the *Middle C Jazz Club* family. We miss no opportunity to, so to speak, jazz up the fund-raising: Sponsorship levels are named for Mel Brooks ($25,000!), Carol Burnett, Louis Armstrong, Joan Rivers, Ella Fitzgerald and, coming in at a modest $1,000, Paul Reiser. Sorry about that, Paul. The Blumenthal award that night will go to some local music entrepreneur named Larry who has always considered it an honor to do his part to help others. The best thing about it is his family will be there to share in his *naches* (Yiddish for pride and joy). The goal is to raise $200,000, a portion of which will go to the Robyn Farber Leadership Development Initiative.

Let me tell you about Robyn.

Robyn lived a tough life. She dealt with asthma and other issues both physical and emotional. And yet her kindness for all people rose above whatever challenges were in her way. Growing up in the Cotswold neighborhood, my sisters Enid (who became an acclaimed jazz photographer) and Robyn shared a bedroom. Robyn (and our parents!) managed to survive all that excitement. One of Robyn's best friends growing up was Maxine Madans – the sister of one of my good friends, Craig Madans. The sight of the Madans family piano changed my life as I shared earlier. Robyn grew up to love unconditionally. She loved pets. She loved the music of Barbra Streisand. She loved her family, especially her maternal grandparents, Poppy and Nanny, who loved her right back.

Robyn was living in an apartment near our dad in Parsippany, N.J., in 1993. We were planning to gather in New Jersey the Friday after Thanksgiving to celebrate her 40th birthday. The Wednesday before Thanksgiving, she was killed by a drunken driver. I will never forget meeting my parents in New Jersey and what my father said at the funeral home. "She's still my baby." The Robyn Farber Leadership Initiative at Temple Beth El helps identify and recruit future leaders of our congregation, then gives them the support and training they need to serve our faith. The same 14 people shouldn't do all the work in a synagogue or any other organization. This initiative aims to deepen the labor pool. May the laborers serve in Robyn's memory. May they be inspired by her pure and simple yearning, that we all love and accept one another. My co-author, Ken Garfield, knows. Just talking about Robyn, he watched as my eyes filled with tears.

Everywhere I turn in my life, I find blessings. I've been privileged to know and be inspired by our congregation's last three senior rabbis – James Bennett, Judy Schindler (who was with me the night Carole King came to town) and Asher Knight. I served on the committees that helped bring us Judy and Asher. I've worked alongside some amazing people to put on all these events. Enthusiastic allies helped and inspired me along the way. Together as we worked, we thanked God for the chance to repair the world. *Tikkun Olam.*

Because collaborating is a sacred act, I must thank those who helped along the way. My deepest apologies if I left anyone out. I've been blessed to have so many cherished friends and partners along the way. Each one helped repair the world.

One For All Ball committee members over the years included Roni Fishkin, Ellen Fligel, Adrienne Gossett, Jonathan Howard, Jill Newman, Lane Ostrow, Allan Oxman, Mitch Rifkin, Anne Sinsheimer, Lynne Sheffer, Lorin Stiefel, Marcy Mehlman, Tammy Menaker and Jill Newman. The National Archives we are not. Forgive me if anyone who helped make these events a hit is not listed. Mickey Gold is co-chairing the *Chai On Laughter & All That Jazz* on Nov. 6. Sara Schreibman, Temple Beth El's awesome former executive director, helped with *Chai On Laughter* as did David Krusch and John Small. The Comedy Zone's Brian Heffron was a gracious host for our comedy fundraisers. Leslie Schlernitzauer of Porcupine Provisions helped feed us deliciously at many gatherings. Tracey Lederer at Temple Beth El helped me with research. Our rabbis and staff at the synagogues and other Jewish institutions have all been an immense encourager to me and the causes I have worked for. Or should I say we have worked for, together?

Larry and Sherri, New Orleans, 2017.

CHAPTER 8
WE ARE FAMILY

My life has never been just about the music. Yes, it's been a thrill to share a moment with Aretha, Tony and other legends. But that's not why I spent so many nights listening to bands and playing music at receptions, clubs and concert halls, immersed in this career. Yes, I wanted to make a comfortable living. But I didn't take a chance on starting a private music club and uptown jazz club to get rich.

I didn't pursue a life representing and booking bands because it's more exciting than examining patients or filing lawsuits, though I believe it is. By a mile. I did this for my family. I did this for the joy of sharing the music with them, passing on my passion to our three sons, instilling in them the values I've tried to live by. Honesty. Persistence (ask anyone who's ever worked with me, I'm good at persistence). No shortcuts. Building lifelong relationships. Giving back to the community. Waking up each day and finding meaning in the work ahead.

I did this to leave a legacy that will make my family proud, that I did something meaningful with my life. My legacy, your legacy whatever that might be, is a treasure worth more than money or acclaim. I hope you see it that way.

I've shared my journey from a kid who played keyboards in The Nightcaps to an agent who once booked a band (Kool & the Gang) for the opening of a luxury hotel in Ethiopia. I saved the best for last. Let me tell you about my family.

It was destined to be, right? My wife, Sherri McGirt, and I met thanks to an entertainment deal.

Back in the early 1980s, I invested $10,000 in a movie, "The Last Game," about a football hero who, you guessed it, wins the last game. The producer, of course, promised us we'd get our money back and more. A bunch of us involved in the movie drove to the premiere. That we didn't fly should have been a tipoff. It was in Shelby, N.C. As we arrived, we ran into a bunch of girls coming out of the theater. They were crying. This was supposed to be a tearjerker. This was a good sign, we thought, until they declared, "We're crying because we had to pay for this." The best part of the movie, if I say so myself, was the soundtrack. I landed Bill Deal & The Rhondels, a popular soul/beach music band back in the day, to provide the music.

What does this have to do with Sherri? Our group wound up suing the guy who made the movie (to no avail). Among the lawyers at Weinstein & Sturges, the firm that represented us? You guessed it.

Sherri and I met for the first time at the law firm's holiday party and shared casual conversation. We began our friendship over lunch. Our first "real" date was to the old P.B. Scott's to see jazz pianist Ramsey

The Farbers, 2016.

Lewis. Early on, she accompanied me to a few gigs and got a taste of what life with me would be like. Despite that (just kidding!), love blossomed. We were married on Sept. 9, 1984. As of this writing, we are at 37 years and counting (our blessings).

We're alike in many ways. We're both from Charlotte. We're both graduates of UNC-Chapel Hill. Sherri appreciates music as much as I do, having played violin at Harding High School and sung in the choir at Myers Park Presbyterian Church. We both love sports. When we were married, she owned a black-and-white TV but no table to put it on. My first gift to her was a color TV and a table so we could watch the Atlanta Braves together.

In other ways, Sherri and I are different. A tax and estate planning lawyer until she retired from Burr & Forman, Sherri is no-nonsense, a wise counsel, a rock in rocky times. No one would say any of those things about me.

Ours is an interfaith marriage. Sherri belongs to Myers Park Presbyterian Church. Temple Bethel is my spiritual home. But rather than a challenge, this has given us an opportunity to express our love for one another by embracing the best of both faiths. Essentially we're all taught to love God and love our neighbors. Period. We wrote our own wedding vows incorporating our two faiths. We wrote our own service – a cross between a baptism and bris (circumcision) – to mark the births of Adam, Harrison and Reid. The secret to an interfaith marriage? I think Sherri and I have hit on it. I say "Jews Don't Camp" (more on this later). She says "No Gefilte Fish In The Refrigerator."

I'll look up at *Middle C* and there Sherri will be with friends, taking in a jazz show. I'll hit a snag in something and there Sherri will be to listen and help.

A family footnote that, of course, includes a story about music: Sherri is close with her brother, Joe McGirt, a retired lawyer, his wife, Carole, their son, Matt, and his sister, Erin. It's Dr. Matt McGirt now. He's 46 years old as of this writing and a prominent neurosurgeon in Charlotte. Remember the baby grand piano Peter Nero signed for me ("Practice, dammit, practice") when I was a kid? It lived for a while at Matt's house when he was young so he could take lessons. Sherri would do anything for Matt. One night back in the 1980s, she and I were headed to see Tina Turner in concert at the old Coliseum on East

Independence Boulevard. Matt, eight at the time, took ill with a sinus infection. His parents were out of town. Aunt Sherri was happy to stay back to babysit him. When I got home, I hated having to tell her that Mick Jagger made a surprise appearance. We all remember that story, Sherri and Matt most of all.

Matt considers himself one of the Farber boys. We consider him one of the boys, too. I asked him to share what life as an honorary Farber was like. Since he's the oldest, as he likes to point out, he gets to go first.

From Matt: "Back in the day, Charlotte was ruled by bankers and Presbyterians. Button-down was the order of the day. Then along came Larry into the family – funny, hip, Hawaiian shirts, all about the music and the joy it can bring us. I remember one Christmas, I was maybe 10, his gift to me was a briefcase. 'A boring briefcase,' I said to myself as I tried to feign excitement for Uncle Larry. Then I opened it and out poured 50 of the best rock albums of the day. When I was in the fifth grade, Larry played keyboards in Now 'n Then. He used to let my friends and me tag along to his band's gigs. We were a cross between roadies and groupies. He'd let us help with the equipment. When the band went on a break, he'd let us play a tune or two. I'm sure we stunk. But hey, we were fifth-graders. We were cute. We were on stage rocking or trying to. It was like we went to the moon on a rocket ship. That's a memory that never fades. One more thing. Sorry about Mick, Aunt Sherri."

Now meet our three sons.

Adam, 35 as I write this, is the oldest. He works in commercial real

Myers Park Trinity Little League, from left, Harrison, Reid, Adam, 1998.

estate with Colliers. Like his brothers, I am proud that he finds ways to reach out to others. Our boys have joined me in support of good causes. Among the ones closest to their heart is Wayfinder, a Charlotte nonprofit that supports students through mentoring and more. Adam's wife, Sarah, is a personal fashion stylist and also works with her parents, Paul and Meredith Bell. They own (majority or minority) some of Charlotte's most popular restaurants – Providence Road Sundries, Lebowski's Neighborhood Grill, The Roasting Company and Eddie's Place. Adam and Sarah have two children, Sutton, 5, and Mac, 2. Those two are tied with their cousin Sam for cutest kids in the world.

All grown up, from left, Reid, Harrison, Adam, 2019.

When they come to our house – we're Pops and Shugie – Sutton loves for me to play the piano. She'll join in and play. It's more like banging though I swear she has the Farber music gene. She already has her favorite Date Night: Going with her dad to *Middle C* and ordering her own small pizza. Mac is the happiest child ever. He loves to dance. Whatever Sutton does, he thinks he has to do, too. The kids' mom, Sarah, is part of the music. She cherishes the photo we took with Aretha Franklin after her *Music With Friends* concert. In it, you can see Aretha clutching that pocketbook filled with cash. Sarah also learned to love the great Bonnie Raitt after seeing her at *Music With Friends*. It was

Sarah's all-time favorite MWF show.

Adam, like our two other boys, graduated from Charlotte Country Day School. He took up piano at an early age and also played trumpet. Adam inherited my love of music and sports. Like me, he worries over his kids, God bless him. He's growing in wisdom. He appreciates the family business and the legacy I hope to leave. Together, we created and opened *Middle C.* We were partners in every sense of the word, with Adam taking the lead on finding the property on South Brevard Street. I know working with me can be intense. That's a polite word for hard. But Adam and I cleared all the hurdles as father and son, then partner and partner. The club is up and running. It's given jazz a home in my town. And it has the Farber name behind it. Two Farbers.

Writing this final chapter, I asked each of the boys to share memories of a family life in music.

From Adam: "Some of my earliest memories are Dad driving carpool, taking my neighborhood friends and me to school. Sorry other parents, but he always played the best music – Earth, Wind & Fire, Michael Jackson, Luther Vandross and more. We nicknamed him The Candy King because he'd take us to Kerr Drugs on Fairview Road after school for snacks and candy. What other kid's dad arranged for Jay Thomas to visit his kindergarten class? I can't believe how my dad can get tickets anytime, anywhere. My brothers and I were in Copenhagen on the day Paul McCartney gave a Fourth of July concert. A couple of calls from Dad and we were in. All the times I got to be in the presence of genius was amazing. I remember shaking hands with Jackson Browne in the stairway at McGlohon Theater. I took my brother-in-

— 116 —

Mac (left) and Sutton Farber, 2021.

law, Tres, to see Steely Dan, one of his all-time favorite bands. I'll never forget the joy it brought him and us. I became social chair of my fraternity, Sigma Nu, at the University of South Carolina. Who better to plan a party than a Farber? I took my wife to see Tony Bennett at *Music With Friends* in Houston. Sarah and I got to listen to him sing a few notes at sound check. Want to impress your wife? Take her to see and hear Tony Bennett at sound check.

"My Dad appreciated people no matter who they are and where they're from. He filled our home with culture and shaped the way we view the world. He taught his sons to think big and pursue what they love. And he gave us music."

I must detour from all this talk about love and legacy to share one of those stories that have become part of Farber lore. Our sons were Boy Scouts, Troop 55 at Myers Park Presbyterian Church. Harrison and Reid made Eagle Scout. It wasn't anything I did. While I was on the road, Sherri was Scout Mom – taking them to meetings, on camping trips and all the rest that goes with it.

On one occasion, she accompanied Adam to the USS Yorktown near Charleston, where the scouts and their dads (and Sherri) were going to camp on the World War II aircraft carrier for the night. When they returned home, not a moment too soon for Sherri, she declared that it was hot, awful and "No more." When it came time for our second child Harrison to camp on the Yorktown, it was my turn. This can't be as bad as Sherri made it out to be, I said to myself (I was too smart to say it to Sherri). About the time the dad at the top of our three-tiered bunk bed passed gas, I climbed out in the dark of night, tiptoed

Four generations of Farbers. Sherri holds Sutton, Adam holds Mac, Larry stands behind his father, Charles, 2020.

over to Harrison, shook him awake and told him to get up, we're going to the Wild Dunes resort nearby to spend the rest of the night in a hotel suite. I also told him to keep this to himself. When we "campers" came home, I recall Harrison took one step inside and reported to Sherri, "Dad and I had the best time on the beach. He woke me up and we went to Wild Dunes." When it came Reid's turn to camp, I went. As soon as the sun rose, we were out of there. They need an 11th Commandment. "Jews (or at least Larry Farber) Shalt Not Camp."

Reid, 27, our youngest, is a booking agent with EastCoast Entertainment. His girlfriend, Lloren Hile, is a gem. A former ICU nurse, she's training to be a nurse anesthetist. To have a child follow in your footsteps, is there a better treasure? Perhaps only when Reid's clients tell me how great he's doing. Reid is organized, builds strong relationships with clients and bands, is driven to be a part of making music and isn't afraid to get up for karaoke. He's the family character. At his two brothers' weddings, he noted in his toast that each had dated their wives for nine years. The longest he's dated anyone, he joked (we hope), is nine minutes. At his brothers' weddings, we also discovered one of his many gifts. He went on stage and rapped as well as any white guy. Inspired by Reid, I, too, rapped at Harrison's wedding rehearsal party. They dubbed me "Kosher Dog."

We almost lost Reid.

He was born at 26½ weeks and weighed two pounds. He spent three months in the Neonatal Intensive Care Unit at Carolinas Medical Center. Either Sherri or I were there 24/7, often both of us, staying with Reid and comforting each other through the difficult days and nights. You know those welcome mats at the hospital that say "Have a nice Monday" and so on? Each day I'd say a prayer to myself, "Let him make it to Tuesday" and so on. I remember Sherri telling me that I have had a lot in luck in life. Could I please extend my luck this one more time?

Luck. The doctors. The grace of God. Who can say from where this blessing came, that we have Reid to love.

From Reid: "When I was five or six, I remember Dad would pop in a Frank Sinatra CD while we were driving and we'd belt out 'New York, New York.' When I was seven or eight, I remember watching

TV, waiting for Dad to arrive home from Alive After Five concerts uptown with all the cash. I'd join everyone at the kitchen table to count it. Since I was a kid, I was in charge of counting the $1 bills. One night, as my dad tells it, I ordered Domino's pizza. Being the friendly kid I was, I invited the delivery guy to bring it into the kitchen – where he saw us huddled around a table full of cash, counting every crumpled bill. No telling who he thought we were and what we did to 'earn' it. When I was 10 or 11, I'd go with my Dad to deliver a check from a gig. We held it up to the light to make sure it was real. Ever since, I always thought that was a cool thing to do. I remember when Luther Vandross died in 2005, sitting in the car with my parents as they listened to a radio station playing his hits. We pulled into the driveway where they spent 30 more minutes marking the loss. I learned the Luther Vandross discography that day. I also learned how music can touch our souls. I think the first concert I attended was James Taylor at what was then Verizon Wireless Amphitheatre. Kenny Mann, the lead singer for Liquid Pleasure, became a friend to all the Farbers. I've heard the stories of how Kenny was on the phone with my dad when I was born prematurely. Kenny had a premature son, too. I've been known to jump on stage with bands. I remember joining one of EastCoast's favorite bands, Black & Blue Experience, and singing 'My Girl' at the engagement party my parents threw for Adam. Hearing legends perform at *Music With Friends* deepened my love of music and helped me find my path in life. To listen to the greatest songwriters talk about the inspiration behind their work in such an intimate setting was priceless. I remember Glenn Frey telling the audience as he stood on stage at

the McGlohon how he and Don Henley came to co-write 'Lyin' Eyes.'
They were sitting at the bar at their favorite West Hollywood restaurant, unknown singer/songwriters at the time, when in walked a beautiful young woman with an older man. He wasn't the best-looking guy
in the place – to say the least – but he was rich. The fact of his wealth,
Frey shared with the audience, couldn't hide what she really felt about
having to go home with him at closing time. *"You can't hide your lyin'
eyes. And your smile is a thin disguise."* As soon as "lyin' eyes" came out
of Frey's mouth, they reached for cocktail napkins because they knew
they had the makings of a hit. When it comes to my dad, I have only
one regret. I wish I would have continued playing the piano so I could
have followed in his footsteps."

Harrison, 32, is our middle son. The boys won't mind me saving him
for last, for a reason you soon will see. He is married to Julia Gray. She's
the daughter of Dr. Tim Saunders, a pediatric ophthalmologist, and Rev.
Lisa Saunders, Associate Rector at Christ Episcopal Church. As with
Adam's in-laws, the Bells, we cherish our friendship with Tim and Lisa.

Harrison played piano and guitar. Like his older brother, it took
Harrison nine years to arrive at the altar with Julia Gray. The two met
at Charlotte Country Day. Julia Gray was 17 and had been dating
Harrison for six months when she discovered a perk to being among
the Farbers. She got to see Gladys Knight at *Music With Friends*. Such
is Julia Gray's scholarly ways, she studied Gladys' music before the
show. I love how Julia Gray puts it, that I take booking a violin quartet
for a bride's walk down the wedding aisle as seriously as I take booking
Darius Rucker for a concert.

— 122 —

— 122 —

CHAPTER 8

The third member of Harrison and Julia Gray's household is Sam. He was born on Jan. 24, 2021, the sixth anniversary of the day his parents got engaged. After Sam's second night home, Harrison sent an urgent plea to the baby's grandparents: PLEASE COME. A sleep-deprived brain surgeon outwitted by an eight-pound human. Sam was five months old when they took him to his first outdoor "concert" – a farmers market with food trucks, dance floor and guitarist playing covers. Sam loved the music. I think he got that from me.

Harrison and Julia Gray are physicians, living and training in Phoenix. He's a neurosurgeon. She's in pediatrics and internal medicine. Our dream is that they one day return to Charlotte to put down roots, personally and professionally. Plan B is to send Sam to live here when he's old enough (assuming he's sleeping through the night by then). Harrison and Julia Gray can come and visit.

Harrison heard the music early. He took piano lessons. He was a roadie for one of my bands, In The Pocket. I remember those gigs. Both of us remember how we'd go for Jack in the Box cheeseburgers at the end of the night. We had a father-son tradition as we rolled up to the drive-through window. I'd ask the poor soul taking our order in the dead of night, "Can you tell me where Jack is?" Harrison would slump down in his seat in embarrassment. A testament to our bond? Harrison kept coming back for more cheeseburgers and his old man's bad jokes.

Each of our boys offered their memories by email. I wasn't prepared for what they shared. Just thinking about it brings tears to my eyes. As the years fly by, you wonder whether you were the best father you could have been. Whether you touched their lives in all the right ways. Whether you touched anyone's life for the better. Then you open your phone and read what your kids have to say about it. I'd like to believe that Harrison, in what he shared, speaks for his brothers.

From Harrison: "My dad's life in music has undoubtedly affected all of us growing up in the Farber family. Music is in our DNA. Some of my earliest memories are taking piano lessons at my house with Daryle Rice and Anne Trenning, my dad going to perform at shows with his band, and stories of all the musicians who came before him in our family. While other kids were listening to Disney and pop radio, we were listening to Luther Vandross and General Johnson. My dad's zeal for music has most affected my life in three ways: Experiences he has given me, experiences he has given others, and cherished memories shared.

"I have so many musical memories thanks to my dad. Once I got to hear one of my favorite songs, 'For Once In My Life,' performed live by Tony Bennett and then Stevie Wonder in the same month. I had dinner with the lead singer of Earth, Wind & Fire, Philip Bailey, after he came off stage from his *Music With Friends* show. Right before the Crosby, Stills & Nash show, I shook hands with Stephen Stills, only to find out he has bad arthritis and my firm handshake caused him to recoil in pain. For about 15 seconds I thought the audience was going to see Crosby & Nash. Thankfully, Stephen, the lead guitarist, was able to play.

"I have always been amazed by the gift my dad is able to give others

Sam Farber, 2021.

The Farbers, 2008.

through his life's work. 'Larry got us our wedding band 20 years ago.' 'We had front row seats to see the Rolling Stones.' These are common refrains I've heard my whole life.

"Lastly, music has given us something to bond over. At the rehearsal party the night before I got married, I asked my dad's band to play. For three songs, we shared the stage. My dad on keys, my future father-in-law on drums and my future brother-in-law and I on guitars. We played for my bride-to-be and weren't half bad. If I wasn't a surgeon maybe I would have been a rock star. Maybe not.

"Most of all, I remember being home and sitting around our baby grand piano together. We could call out most any jazz, Motown or pop song and chances are he could play it. On Christmas morning, he'd play Christmas songs while we opened presents. Sometimes he would play a set of chords and Reid and I would figure out how to play piano solos on top of them. We might sit there playing for an hour or more.

"My dad dares to dream big and relentlessly carries on until his ideas are reality. For a guy who is pretty anxious at baseline, he sure does thrive on stress and overcoming challenges. While my career path is vastly different than his, I don't fail to recognize how his attributes have molded me. His tireless work ethic, ability to overcome adversity, genuine care for others and commitment to his calling are all traits I try to emulate in my own life. I hope my example will affect my children as much as he has affected me."

What Harrison wrote in that email?
That's why I set out on this journey.

So that's my story.
I saw the baby grand piano in the home of my childhood friend and knew where I was headed.
I found true love in Sherri and our family.
I spent a lifetime sharing the music.
I dared to dream about a private music club, then a jazz club.
I appreciated the value of relationships, whether it was a band I represented, a bride I did business with or a friendship I had with a funny

guy named Jay Thomas.

I savored my encounters with the world's most gifted artists, not for the brush with fame but for the moments spent with genius.

I tried to give back to my synagogue and community, remembering as I did my sister Robyn.

As I grew old, my step slowed, but that gave me time to linger with grandchildren.

I put it all in these pages, hoping that when the last note rings, the grandchildren and everyone else who graced my life will know the story and carry it on.

NOTED MEMORIES
Available in paperback and Kindle version for
$25 plus tax (and shipping when applicable)

- Amazon and elsewhere online.

- Park Road Books at Park Road Shopping Center, Charlotte. (704) 525-9239. www.parkroadbooks.com.

- Discovered Traditions Gift Shop at Temple Beth El, 5101 Providence Road, Charlotte. (704) 749-3060. www.templebethel.org.

- Middle C Jazz Club, 300 S. Brevard St., uptown Charlotte. (704) 595-3311. www.middlecjazz.com.

- Music With Friends. (704) 607-3937. Available at each show.

- You can also email surquhsrt@middlecjazz.com to order a copy.

Partial sales from the book will support *Arts Plus*, a Charlotte-based nonprofit that sponsors arts education for students of all ages, skill levels and socioeconomic backgrounds. Learn more at (704) 377-4187 or www.artsplus.org.

Partial sales from "Noted Memories" will support *Arts Plus*, a Charlotte-based nonprofit that offers arts education to students of all ages, skill levels and socioeconomic backgrounds. It formerly was known as Community School of the Arts. Programs include music and visual arts camps, private lessons and group classes on a variety of topics, among them "Discovering Suzuki" for young children and "Comic Book Drawing" for young adults and up. Its mission: "Unleashing creativity, transforming lives and building community through outstanding and accessible arts education."

345 N. College St. (704) 377-4187. www.artsplus.org.

THANK YOU

Thank you for your interest in my story.
Want to learn more about our musical ventures?

Music With Friends
(704) 607-3937
www.musicwithfriends.com/charlotte

Middle C Jazz Club
300 S. Brevard St., Charlotte
(704) 595-3311
www.middlecjazz.com

CPSIA information can be obtained
at www.ICGtesting.com
Printed in the USA
BVHW040137241021
619367BV00009B/17